PARIZAD SHAIKH

ISBN
Paperback 979-8-89610-725-5
Hardcase 979-8-89632-389-1

Disclaimer

The incidents stated in this book are purely of the author and her friend Pal and bear no resemblance or link to anyone.

The author has through this book expressed solely her solicited views on the subject.

Contents

About the Author

I was born and raised in India, and currently residing in Australia for a couple of years now.

I am a professor in one of the top Australian Universities and I am a double Bachelors, double Masters, and a PhD. I am also a Professional Healer and Author of a book named 'Kimaya.'

I have launched my own company 'Divine Gifts' in India and Australia and aim to successfully spread it over the world.

Acknowledgement

I wish to extend my thanks to all those who I have come across and who gave me these stories to narrate.

My inspiration for authoring this book is my friend Pal, and the countless people who are seeking partners in marriage. I thank all of you as your unique experiences might shape how people approach marriages in the future.

I thank my parents & family for their immense love and support.

Lastly, I thank Kimaya who has been my divine gift all this while.

Introduction

My name is Parizad Shaikh. I am divorced and approached with proposals.

I have a childhood friend named Pal who is 28 years old, unmarried, and looking out for partners.

We are considered the less fortunate girls/women by society. Why? Since society has set norms that a girl of marriageable age should compulsorily get married to a guy and settle down, so she can be happy. Despite the proposal being her choice or not.

Furthermore, a divorcee should definitely find herself a partner who can protect her, regardless of whether she wants to remarry or not.

We are classified as the 'UNMARRIED.'

As humans, most of us want to have partners in some form or the other, and then it is the law of nature. We are social beings, and society has created its fences - the so-called laws.

Pal has faced men who thought she was past her prime age for marriage, suggesting,

"Who will marry you now at this age?" On the other hand, there's my experience with marriage proposals as a divorcee. I encountered suitors with a biased mindset, stating, "If I don't marry you, no one else will, because of your marital status." The contrasting experiences highlight the unique challenges faced in the quest for love and companionship.

I'm certain that many people find themselves in the same boat, facing significant setbacks on their journey to marriage. Many remain voiceless or are silenced by societal and parental pressures. In countless cases it becomes worse, with situations forcing them to suffer in silence or make compromises.

In this book, I share with you some of my own experiences, and others belong to my childhood friend Pal. Together, we have been able to navigate this marriageable phase for Pal with hope, faith, values, love, and learnings.

For everyone reading this book, know that hope is within reach. The best is yet to come, and when it does, there will be no room for ifs and buts. Be vigilant and thoughtful in your quest for a life partner.

I am sure you will have your own experiences, while some of you might have similar experiences like ours. We are sharing our experiences so everyone reading this book can reflect on the things happening in their life and stand up for themselves to find the perfect match.

The idea is to committedly pursue your dreams for an 'ALMOST PERFECT' match and keep looking until you find your *'Almo - The Almost Perfect Partner.'*

Chapter 1
Kimaya

Adain with his sunflower eyes was mesmerizing. I fell in love with him and seem to have never come out of it. It's been almost 20 years now. While we dated for eight years and had a short-married life of just six months.

I was caught off guard by this storm that hit my life. Just after separating from my husband, and reeling under that shock, another irreversible storm struck me. I was told I was pregnant, only when I had a miscarriage. I couldn't even tell my husband because he accused me of having an extra marital affair. The man I stood by through thick and thin for eight years would no longer believe it was his own baby. It felt like I was in an abyss, and then life could not get any worse than this.

From a fairy tale romance to marriage, to divorce, and then facing a miscarriage all alone, I found myself spiralling into depression. I believed our love was strong enough to weather any storm, to overcome all obstacles and societal pressures. What went missing was the commitment, our declining communication, and the overwhelming pressure of society on a new daughter-in-law towards fulfilling all her duties.

Post-divorce, what continued to unfold were the various proposals that came my way. Some of them labelled me as a divorcee, seemingly ready to marry me with an attitude of doing me a great Favor. Yet, throughout I held out hope for Adain. The struggle was real, and the wait was long.

My wedding cost me 20 lakhs and my divorce 50 lakhs, whatever, both were worth it finally.

I have been able to explore myself to the fullest after my divorce. I have continued my studies and have become a double graduate, a double masters and a PhD holder. Although it cost me a fortune, I am glad I made a sound investment - in myself.

I was happy. Whoever said money can't buy happiness, clearly did not pay for a divorce. I am independent and have travelled to new countries and met new people for my education and work. It took me time to balance myself and get back on my feet, and I did it. It was worth every penny.

Eventually, I will remarry, however there's still time now. It is a conscious choice that I have made.

My first book, 'Kimaya' is my memoir. It delves into the intricacies of my love life, the subsequent divorce, my journey toward self-discovery and reclaiming my self-esteem.

Chapter 2
Childhood

Pal and I go back a long way. We were not just friends; we were a two-people gang. There had been no day in our childhood that we were not together. After coming from our schools, we used to spend our maximum time with each other, playing, doing our homework until our parents would call us for dinner, which again we often ended up doing at each other's place. We were like two peas in a pod, always comfortable in each other's presence. We were inseparable and the reason was we just naturally fitted into each other's aura.

Pal had a gift of being clairvoyant. Pal was the more informed one. She could sense and see things that could happen in the future. She was sensitive to people and their aura, and how they responded to her. Even as a child, her clairvoyance was strong. She had received this divine power from her parents who were also gifted. Growing up her parents informed her about how most people are not gifted and yet might not understand the worth or relevance of your special ability. Therefore, you need to guard it well, and not make it known to anyone unless needed. Hence, Pal did not disclose her divine gift to anyone.

She was aware of the people and their energies even as a child, and through our conversations she had understood that I was aligned with her. I naively told her about my dreams, and she interpreted them knowing I carry her special gift too. I too was informed but unaware. Pal knew it and she never told me about my powers. I had an uncanny quality of knowing things in advance. As a child I had predicted events, sometimes someone's death, birth, sex of an unborn child, marriages, and critical health conditions. There were also instances where I could see my exam question papers in advance. I would go on to see the failure of my marriage also, just two days before my wedding.

We were after all children, and our maximum effort was spent playing. As we grew, Pal realized my dreams were becoming more distinct and were coming to life.

When I told her about the trident (*trishul*) birthmark on my forehead and how my family members kept saying, "She is God's child,"

Pal often asked me to show it to her. I cleared my forehead of my fringes and showed her the mark that had faded over time as I grew up. She trusted me, and what I said. That was the camaraderie we had built even as children. Pal and I both had many friends, although between us we had a different level of connection where we understood each other even without saying things. We were Siamese twins with different bodies.

Life is not always what we envision. Pal and I had a flavor of it at a very tender age. One fine day, Pal's dad disclosed that they are shifting to another city to start his new business.

We were just nine years old when we separated, I handed her a passport-sized photo of mine in an emerald frock. Even as children we knew that these ways of the world are not just taking us away from each other, going forth they would leave a big gap in our life. Back then, our attachment was only over our games, toys, and spending time with each other. Somewhere we were not aware that we had a bigger role to play in each other's life. What and how, was to unveil only as we grew up.

In hindsight, I see that Pal has been sent into my life with a purpose. As kids we were separated due to her father's decision to relocate, and we started living our individual lives. We were adding numbers to our age. Being in different cities and in responsibilities, we were separated by fate.

During my college days I found a person whom I loved so much that my entire life circled around him. I was oblivious of everything around now. His presence kind of brought a hurricane into my life. I was just getting deeper and deeper in the vortex unaware. I did not think much about Pal then. We were too alienated to share what was going on in our lives. I didn't even have contact with her and lived in a faint memory that someone such existed for me once.

Over time, I was preoccupied with the storms that hit me. Perhaps Pal was busy making her career and settling in with her stuff.

However, there came a time when Pal started getting visions about me. She started having dark dreams like I was in a graveyard; at other times she saw I was surrounded by snakes. Once she saw my silhouette being overpowered by lightning and dark energy. This kept repeating and there came a time when she decided to fathom the reason behind her glimpses.

From her clairvoyance she was sure that I was in some danger and needed help. However, we were not connected and that was the reason she could not reach out to me just about immediately.

Pal asked her father if he had any contact with my dad. She tried finding me on social media. Because of my marital issues I had been estranged from it and had deleted all my accounts. Pal was desperate to reach me, and she made many attempts to find me.

Finally, her father traced my father's number and by that time Pal had a job in Mumbai.

The first thing she did was to call my mom and check if we stayed at the same place and not to mention that she called me.

One fine day she just dropped in at my place and surprised me. I couldn't gather who she was on seeing her. She threw a lot of hints at me. Unfortunately, I remained clueless. When I was all ready to give up and offer my early goodbyes to her stating, I am busy playing your guessing games Mam, she sensed my disinterest and gradually took out something from her purse. She handed me a photo which was old. When I looked at it, my eyes glowed. It was my childhood photo in the emerald frock which I had given to her as we were parting.

As I saw that photo, I jumped on Pal and hugged her hard. It took us days to update on the years we remained unheeded to each other. We had to catch up on so many things. We had to ask, differ, cry, fight, hug and support each other.

Finally, I laid bare my love and brief married life to her, and she told me about her trials with finding a good guy for marriage. She thought arranged marriage was for her, and would say, "who said, it's easy."

"Why is that so?" I inquired. I was someone who never went that lane with a stable love relationship for eight years followed by a failed marriage with the same guy.

Pal mentioned, "It's difficult because it is not just the girl, and the boy involved in an arranged marital relationship. Instead, it's their parents and sometimes their extended families too. The couple is just the face of the relationship, although the decisions are taken by the elders in the family, and often ruled by their expectations."

"Whereas, after my experience I now feel, the decision should be taken by the couple and not their families," I claimed.

I continued, "How does that matter? Elders come into picture in love marriages too."

Pal mentioned, "Whatever, it's all pre-decided in love marriages. The elders only come to give consent and make arrangements."

"For me, it's always love marriage. I would feel haunted marrying a stranger, going to a new house, and spending my time in a closed room with a person I do not know. I do not want anyone to interfere in my relationship. My partner's entire family was involved in my marriage, but no help came to me during my divorce. I wish there was no extra interference then.

So now, I am strong enough to handle myself and not have any external factors interfering in my life." I responded.

"Why do you say that Pari?" Pal asked.

"Pal, my married life was challenged because of a third person. I suffered because someone in my acquaintances had a not so good motive." I replied sadly.

"Why, what happened?" Pal asked looking into my eyes.

"I haven't told you about Andrew. Or have I?" I asked intensely.

Chapter 3
The Jealous Lover

Adain and I loved each other for a long time before we decided to get married. Yet, amidst this lovely feeling, lurked Andrew, a person who coveted my affection. He was blinded by his own desires. He was besotted with me and thought of every way to claim me in his life.

From the moment Andrew laid eyes on me, his life's purpose was to marry me. Although he was aware of my commitment to Adain. Despite my gentle refusals and loyalty to Adain, Andrew persisted, his desperation clouded his judgment.

Time and again, Andrew attempted to approach me with his marriage proposal, promising me of lavish vacations and material wealth, albeit my heart, my love was only for Adien. Andrew was finally frustrated seeing my unwavering decision.

As my wedding day to Adain drew near, Andrew's desperation reached a fever pitch. Confronting me with his ultimatums, he vowed to sabotage my happiness if I dared to reject him. Yet, I stood resolutely unaware of what Andrew was up to.

As the day of my wedding approached, Andrew's obsession took a darker turn. In a final act of defiance, Andrew proposed to my cousin for marriage. I knew his intentions were shrouded in malice and deceit. Though I should have felt relief at his decision, I couldn't shake the ominous feeling that Andrew's sinister plans extended far beyond.

Despite the rejection, Andrew had a masterstroke. He planted a seed of deception that I am not trustworthy, and that eventually led to the fall of my marriage in six months. In the end, Adain burnt down the house for a rat which didn't even exist.

I had given up on the thought of remarriage entirely because of my experiences. Love or arranged, it seems marriage as a system sucks.

Pal denied saying, "Look at our parents, they are living examples of well-established and successful marriages."

I remarked, "True. Perhaps, I am the one who is overwhelmed and running from this institution called marriage. For me true love matters above all."

Chapter 4
The Bridesmaid

In Indian society it is mandatory that a girl should get married at a particular age, educated or not. It is a longstanding wish of all parents to see their girl married and settled, as if that is the only task they have been entrusted on this earth- The act of doing *Kanyadaan* - giving the daughter in marriage being the most sacred one in India.

Pal's parents started seeking proposals for her. Their desire was to see her married. However, Pal mentioned they do not have any restrictions on me, because they know I am wise enough to make decisions and that I will consult them when the right match comes along.

Pal and I started discussing marriage prospects in her office as she was just getting started on the journey of marriage. I had witnessed a full circle- affair, marriage, and divorce and was far from the prospect of marriage. Nevertheless, I did not want to dissuade Pal, as she had her new journey to start. She was hopeful and expected a lot out of marriage. Maybe she is right on her part. I have some bitter experiences, and thus my approach is different.

I often under my blanket of dejection felt like warning her of the effects of marriage. At the end, her enthusiasm only made me support her in this endeavour called marriage.

Pal started telling me instances from her office encounters. It was a chronicle of events and experiences, and she seemed happy narrating them. I was a good listener, and she had her friend back after years. We were beginning to be each other's strength and support again to witness a new part of our life together.

I suggested to Pal, "Before you marry a person, you should first make them drive with you in a car at 60 kms in a 100 kms speed zone during your office hours, without honking.

I wish the pre-nuptials had behavioral, social, physical, psychological, and financial criteria. This would take care of the different dynamics in a relationship post marriage and if people were educated about all these things, there would be less marriages, or informed marriages resulting in less chaos and fewer children. The world would be a less populated place, and certainly much more sorted."

Pal exclaimed, "I wonder about the different expectations men have towards their marriage partner. People come around with various expectations – some talk about skin colours, some about dowry, some about status, and in all this very little attention is given towards the girl's dreams and ambitions. They are in fact not driven by any goal. Their agenda is just to have the title of 'Married.' While the man continues to be in his league and does what he wants to. Very little insight is sought about the girl. She is just expected to be some man's wife and serve the man's family. Having a career is a second or sometimes no choice at all for the girl."

*"Clothes make the man. Naked people have little or no influence in society." I exclaimed, "*Pal, our clothes are our status, good looks, money and how well-known we have been. Power plays a different level game. Where's your ticket to all this girl?

Superior males have an attitude, and they feel that I am doing a favour for womankind. Rather, if we do not marry women, who will?"

Over the months, Pal and I were in touch daily and kept meeting regularly, and after our discussions Pal figured out that I was withdrawn and being cautious of relationships. Especially after my divorce I had given up on men. I was not attempting to meet men or was thinking of remarrying. I was dead as a doornail. Pal after seeing my condition wanted me to come out of my current state. She was already looking for proposals, and now she asked me to accompany her to every meeting she could have with a prospective groom. Although she told me she would like to have my opinion of the boy, deep down I knew she wanted me to move out, socialize, and get back to normal. She couldn't see me in such a withdrawn state. She thought I was too young to give up on life, and the pleasure of meeting people and enjoying life.

I could not deny her, because I wanted to support her in any and every way I could. I agreed to be there at as many meetings as she had with a new proposal. We decided to meet these proposals in a nearby café we both frequented. The best part was the café staff were well acquainted with us as we started going there together. Having a secure place to meet the guys, we knew we could concentrate on other things now.

Pal, "Why are you going for an arranged marriage? Are you not in love with anyone? Is there no decent guy in your office who you like or has proposed to you?"

"I'm playing it safe, not trying to jump out of the frying pan into the fire," Pal remarked, "office romance is a tough nut to crack and often more trouble than it's worth. I've always kept my nose to the grindstone, maintaining a highly professional profile in the office, and I don't want to muddy the water for any reason. Although once I was almost put to the test."

"Ouu!! What happened?" I asked, my curiosity piqued.

"Let's have some popcorn ready. It's time to spill the beans," she uttered, leaning in dramatically.

Chapter 5
The Horny Gentleman

"This guy was a software developer in my office. He was onsite for our US process, and then stationed in my office. Through chance we met at a common friend's party where we were introduced. Soon we found ourselves drawn to each other's company. Our conversations flowed effortlessly, traversing the world of technology, philosophy, and the ever-evolving world around us.

We maintained a close connection, chatting regularly irrespective of the different time zones of Mumbai and the bustling tech hub of America. Our virtual conversations were like a bridge over international waters, keeping us connected despite the distance. He was a man with a radiant spirit, and cheerful. His presence illuminated the room with warmth. His hoarse voice carried infectious enthusiasm, drawing people to him. His genuine, ever-present smile radiated joy, lifting even the heaviest of hearts. Tall, well-built, and fair, he exuded strength and vitality, carrying himself with confident humility.

A man of many passions, he was always eager to explore new knowledge and experiences. His boundless curiosity and insatiable zest for life made our encounters filled with laughter, heartfelt conversations, and the excitement of discovery.

Movies beckoned us, and we would go watch Hollywood movies with colleagues. He was cheerful, and full of life. Someone who would make me smile. I looked forward to meeting him as a friend. Marriage - I was apprehensive about him as a life partner.

Yet, as we got pally, he casually yet persistently started inquiring about my attire hinting at his expectations of a more culturally diverse attire. He would ask, "Do you wear skimpy clothes? I have always seen you dressed in formals?"

My initial inability to understand his intentions stemmed from my perception of our relationship as a close friendship. I viewed his comments as harmless observations, unaware of the deeper meaning he might have intended.

As our interactions continued, I gradually began to read between the lines and recognize the unspoken desires underlying his remarks.

I discerned that his expectations of seeing revealing dresses on me were not merely about fashion. It was about a level of intimacy that he expected from me beyond our friendship.

I thought, having spent time in the US, he may have been accustomed to a more casual and physically expressive culture, where a revealing attire was often associated with openness and receptivity. I was conscious of my office surroundings and was not dressing for anyone but for my work. Although this comment stuck with me, I did not respond to him. I realized that he has been in the US for a long time. It's just a cultural thing for him and I should not pay much attention to it. Despite these differences, we shared a genuine connection as buddies.

One sunny afternoon, we colleagues went to a Hollywood movie in a theatre. He found a place beside me. As the film unfolded, a scene played out that seemed to catch his attention. In an unsettling moment, he leaned in and whispered to me, 'She has cum.'

My naivety prevented me from comprehending the suggestive nature of his words. Perplexed, I turned to him and asked, 'What does that mean?' Unfazed, he responded with a cryptic offer, 'I can show it to you, then explain.'

I was uncomfortable with the sudden change of energy, his coyote smile and felt a sense of unease creeping in. It was evident that there was not just a cultural gap between us but a moral gap too. The clash between my conservative values and his seemingly casual approach to intimacy left me feeling out of place.

He was persistently hinting at the prospect of physical intimacy. Following the movie, we all went to a well-known local beach. As we strolled along the shore, he made a nasty comment on a lady's figure who had just emerged from bathing in the sea.

I retorted, 'You should be back in the US. Trust me, it's not acceptable here, your sleazy comments.'

He then shocked me further. With a grin he asked, 'Ok, you are jealous!! If you say, I will show you how to cum. I can show you all that is acceptable and unacceptable.' Hearing this I lost my cool.

I replied shocked, 'Whatever you want to tell me acceptable or not, tell me here, in front of all.'

All my colleagues and the people on the beach froze at my sudden and loud outburst and looked at us. I said agitated, 'When you are a friend, stay within your limits. Don't cross your boundaries.'

I continued, 'The very first time when I did not respond to your advances clearly meant it's a No. Instead, you persisted.'

He appeared flustered, having eventually agreed with my perspective on the nature of our relationship. He was sure about what he wanted, and I was firm about my decision. He did not throw any argument or justify or even convince me. Never apologized even. He knew this was not working the way he wanted and it's better to back off.

I learnt; everybody has their priorities. While some look for meaningful relationships, some might just need to talk a lot, some might look for long-term engagement, others might just need a fling to pass time. This guy was sure he wanted nothing beyond a physical relationship. While my goal was clear, his goal too was super clear. We nowhere had anything in common, and thus it was better to go our separate ways."

Pal hushed herself as if she had finally crossed the winning line and relaxed after running a marathon.

I declared, "Your gentleman was horny. Had I been in your place, I would have drifted him off alone in the deep sea, without any life support and asked him to CUM at his own liberty."

And we both laughed aloud.

Pal explained, "That's two people put in one - Horny and Gentleman are the rarest combinations."

"Babes, your vagina deserves someone better," I claimed.

Pal winked at me and shared, "It's strange how people can paint such a perfect picture at first, only to reveal their different layers over time."

"I'm really glad you nipped it in the bud. In a close-knit office like yours, rumours could spread like wildfire. I'm proud of you for handling it so well. Now your colleagues will not have stories cooked behind your back. They have witnessed it all themselves," I replied.

Pal shared, "Yes, we had awkward confrontations after that, being in the same office. However, good that he is onsite again."

"Yeah, the expectations play a big role and that's where the mismatch happens. It's good to be careful, and not venture deep very soon in relationships. It hurts, eventually. Good he respected your decision after all." I mentioned.

"Yes. Indeed," Pal answered.

"Pal, there are people who are very insensitive and do not care beyond their expectations. It so happened to me..." I narrated.

Chapter 6
The Insensible Guy

"There was a death in my immediate family, and we were all shook to the core because of it. Losing a close family member was a grave situation and we just didn't know how we would be able to live after this loss. We were all emotionally drained and looking for some way our person would come back to us. Thinking it was all a bad dream.

On the third day of the demise, a guy in our acquaintance messaged my Dad stating he wants to marry my Dad's daughter. Now this was a very confusing message, as my father has three daughters. Secondly, we were not in a state of mind to entertain any such people or proposals. My dad did not revert for the first time.

The guy did not stop there. After not receiving any revert from my Dad, he messaged my family members about his interest in marrying me. No one responded as if we all were not in that frame of mind. The guy did not even empathize with our condition. How he was insensitive to what we were going through.

This time he messaged me directly and I lost my calm.

I decided to strike him off directly by meeting him. I texted him to meet me at my regular coffee shop.

He had proved his insensitiveness already. When I went to meet him, he confirmed his immaturity. He came across as a very dominant person. Seems my initiative towards meeting him made him feel that I had accepted his marriage proposal already. He was unaware that he was in for some big trouble.

He was so confident that I am going to say yes to him, that he had already made his plans. He had already decided my destiny and scripted my future. Like everything will happen as he had planned.

He suggested, 'You can wear any kind of clothes with me, but in front of my parents, you have to drape a dupatta on your head.'

I mentioned, 'I dress western, and will not wear clothes to impress anyone. Nobody tells me what to wear and what not to.'

I had my BOLD CAPS LOCK mode on. There was no way he could have his say with me.

He then asked me, 'Do you know how to drive? I want to sit beside you, while you drive.'

I didn't even feel like I deserved to answer this guy or sit there and face him. In the end here I was to protect my family's sanity from this insensitive guy. I coldly replied, 'Although I drive, I have learnt driving only as a skill. I have been driven by drivers.'

He neglected what I said and declared, 'I have already told my dad that I am going to marry you only.'

I asked him in an intense tone, coming straight to the point, 'Did you even ask for my consent?'

He enthusiastically reported, 'I have already asked your father.'

I chuckled and asked, 'So, did he give consent? After all, my consent matters. My Dad will never go out of my word.'

His approach was, 'We will see!!'

I could not control my devilish laugh, and then looked straight in his eyes and replied, 'I saw, and my answer is a definite no. I am not interested in marrying you. So kindly please leave us alone in this sad time.'

He was still confident that my Dad would not listen to me. He was of the mindset who feels that girls don't have any say in taking decisions. Well, he did not know how evolved my family is.

In two days, the guy messaged my Dad again stating, 'I am coming home with my parents to offer condolences.' My father confirmed this.

When he came home with his parents, His father asked to meet me too. I was not interested in seeing his parents, although I went out of respect. After all, they were guests at our place. I went to the living room where they all sat with my father.

The guy's father gave me a cursory glance which I did not like. He then asked me, 'How educated are you?'

This question startled my father and me. They were here for condolence, right? I looked at my father wondering why that strange question was in a condolence meeting.

'I have done masters,' I replied instantly, ignoring what the question actually meant.

My father immediately interrupted, 'All my daughters and son are very well educated.'

The guy's father replied, 'My son has been following up with you so much for marriage. Get married to my son, or no one else would marry you.'

He was obviously not happy with my answer and indicated, 'You are a divorcee, and you do not have many options. You might as well accept my son's proposal.'

I was fuming and in a heated voice asked, 'Uncle, no one talks to me like this. Mind your words when talking to me this way.

Even if he is the last person on earth, and I am not dying to get married, I will never say yes, this way. And let me tell me, you and your son are imposing your decision one me.

Moreover, why is your son hell bent on marrying a divorcee? Don't marry!! Nobody does a favour by getting married, let me make this crystal clear.'

In a clear voice and stable tone, I politely declined as I announced, 'I am not interested in marrying your son. I had already given him my answer, and hope it is clear to everyone now.'

I felt this person has come into my life to test my anger management skills. I was so ready with my boxing gloves on, standing opposite him in the ring, ready to fight, but patiently waited for his first move so I could knock him down. I was very anguished by this experience. My parents also observed the scorn in the person's voice, like he was here to seal my destiny with his son.

In the end my Dad intervened, 'My daughter has conveyed her reply. You are no one to come to our place and talk to my daughter like this. I am sure of not giving my daughter in a family where people have such closed thoughts and mindset. My daughter is independent and confident. Your son will need one more life to match her accomplishments. Thanks for being part of our mourning. You can leave now.'

Pal, they were definitely not the people, or the family I want to be married to. My parents always supported me and respected my individuality." Saying, I finally took a breath.

"I understand Pari, the world is a wonderful place to be, you only have to deal with some narcissists, or assholes who lack basic common sense," Pal remarked.

"Common sense is like a fart, Pal. You are attuned to your own, but others find it disgusting. This one was a disgusting fart," I declared, and we laughed out loud.

"Jokes apart Pal, seriously I think this guy was trying to make use of my family's emotional state in this period of loss. Seems he felt that, as the family is grieving, they might want to have some good things happen sooner, and we might easily say yes to the proposal. That they were doing us a favour by extending a proposal in such times."

Pal readily mentioned, "Having said that I remember this proposal. OMG, this was the person who made me feel like he had come to birth to make my life a better place. That I would be doomed if I don't marry him."

I was curious and uttered, "Tell me then...."

Chapter 7
The Celibate Guy

"There was this guy from the outskirts of Mumbai, I met through a friend's recommendation. He was seeking a partner for marriage. He had his own software development business. His profile showed that he had been interested in religious activities and had a traditional approach to life.

Apart from his religious pursuits and software expertise, he had a knack for reading astronomical charts. This eclectic mix of interests suggested he was a jack of all trades, someone who appreciated both the spiritual and the scientific sides of life.

As we exchanged messages, his connection to his cultural roots became much more apparent. I have had a modern outlook on life and was curious about how these traditional values intertwined with his software business.

Despite being in different cities, we began to hit it off online, and our connection grew stronger. We often found ourselves chatting away for hours. One day, he invited me to visit his house.

What I saw knocked my socks off and left me itching to know more.

He lived in an ancestral house, a grand structure with an old-world charm. Towers adorned the surroundings, and his house stood a silent witness to the passage of time. It was situated in one of the finest localities. I couldn't help but marvel at the historical and architectural significance of the place.

Intrigued by the choice of staying in such an old house, I asked him, 'Why do you choose to stay in an ancestral house?"

He mentioned, 'Lucrative offers, amounting to crores, were being made for the prime land the house stood on. Even in the hustle and bustle of this fast-growing city, I have a profound connection to this ancestral property. It's worth many crores. I chose to preserve the heritage that is part of my family's legacy. The house holds sentimental value. It is not merely a property; it has my familial roots. It is my father's and my wish to preserve our ancestral home.'

'After marriage, would you still stay in this house?' I asked, a bit sceptical. 'I'd always lived in a modern flat with all the bells and barricades, and everything at the click of a button. I was surrounded by neighbours and lived in a well-guarded society. Your place, on the other hand, is a standalone ancient house that didn't show any trace of my lifestyle. I was trying to be down-to-earth and forward-thinking and couldn't help but voice my concerns. In the long run, the house might face structural challenges and could come crashing down. To my mind, accepting the substantial offers for the land seems like a pragmatic choice.'

He responded, 'I get the challenges of maintaining an old structure, but this is my home, and this is where I want to stay.'

'As we're thinking on the lines of tying the knot, it's only natural that you'd want to know where we'd live after marriage. My intention behind this home tour was to show you the ropes. I need a homemaker who can take care of this house, maintain it, keep it strong and run it along with me. I need someone who can roll with the punches and be ready to stay where I do.'

Soon, we started a discussion on astrology and horoscopes. He asked me for my birth details and offered that he would give me a brief idea about what my life is going to look like. He in a contemplative tone revealed that his parents held conservative views and insisted on the traditional practice of matching horoscopes before considering a marriage proposal.

'So, what do our horoscopes say?' I inquired excitedly.

With a hint of hesitancy, he disclosed a significant revelation – 'Our horoscopes do not match. In fact, my horoscope says, I am advised against marriage. My astronomical charts suggest a life of celibacy.'

'Why didn't you mention your celibacy status earlier? You've been reading your charts all along. How is it that you know about it only now? I'm sure I'm not the first girl you've spoken to about marriage. We have been talking all this while, you never mentioned this. Why did you keep this from me?' I demanded, my voice thick with frustration and disbelief.

The revelation about his newly discovered celibate status hit me like a ton of bricks, leaving me hurt and questioning the authenticity of our connection. His response was marked by silence, as if he'd been caught with his hand in a hinge, unprepared for the disclosure of his internal thought process.

His justification was a candid admission, 'The fact is, you are *Manglik* (Having the Mars defect). As per astrology, marriage between a Manglik and Non-Manglik is said to be short-lived and so we cannot get married. However, despite the odds, I am ready to marry you.'

'And why would you do that favour on me? What about your parents and their consent?' I asked, apprehensively.

'Because Mangliks have difficulty getting married. You might face many challenges with the astrology chart you have," he replied. "I can protect myself through some poojas and crystals, because I have learned astrology.'

His words continued to hit me like a sledgehammer, leaving me questioning the very foundation of our connection and the true intentions behind his actions. This unexpected turn of events shattered me making me wonder about his real intentions now.

His statement of me being a Manglik struck a chord. Coming from a Hindu background where a child's horoscope is made at the time of birth, my parents had been to astrologers several times with my birth chart, and even I had shown my horoscopes before too. No astrologer told me I am a Manglik.

I decided to dig into the matter, as I felt I was being framed into something I was not.

Marriage is not just spiritual communion, it is also about washing the dishes and doing the laundry by taking turns, I thought. It is about straight communication and clarity not just about maintaining home and families. It is about individuality and yet dependability.

His message was crystal clear to me — perhaps, he wanted to marry me, and by claiming me as the weaker partner. For someone who can be so manipulative, is it worth hitching my wagon to his for life?

Frankly, I've heard that horoscopes can influence human relationships, however only up to a point. While they might warn you of possible outcomes, they don't hold the key to lasting relationships. What really makes relationships endure is mutual trust, reliance, and commitment. If both partners are dedicated, transparent, and loyal, giving their all to the relationship, I'm sure the results will be far more splendid than any horoscope could predict."

"Pal, did he predict your afterlife? If not let me make a prediction - you are going to be very busy in your afterlife haunting such people." I exclaimed.

"Any doubt about that." Pal laughed and answered.

After this episode, I decided that I had to go to an astrologer and recheck my astrological chart.

"Clean it shows. No Manglik status, the astrologer assured." Pal confirmed.

At the second astrologer, I accompanied Pal. He asked, "Who told you that you are a Manglik? Seems someone very naïve and uninformed about how to read the charts."

Pal looked at me and expressed, "That's what happens when you use your hobby to make life decisions."

"Especially when you are clueless about something, people misuse that piece of information and use it against you. I can't believe the lengths some people will go to for marriage or to turn someone down." I remarked.

"He was trying to say he was doing me a favour by sacrificing himself in the name of celibacy. Perhaps he was trying to play the hero by not wanting to hurt me with his claim that I was Manglik, which I wasn't? What fun is it?" Pal mentioned sarcastically. "Does he feel there is no option left for me? That my life is over because I am a Manglik. Now, who will marry me, if not him?" Pal was still fuming.

"He was acting as if he had all the answers. Like he was God's gift to women. The storm that will disrupt everything on the way yet can protect only you. Nevertheless." Pal continued.

"Buddy don't worry, because it's over. Smile because the dude is nobody's problem as he has to lead a celibate life. Men-O-Men," I sighed.

Pal mentioned an idea that struck her, "I don't want to be fooled by anyone henceforth. I want to learn astrology. I will. Why don't you learn it with me too? It's nothing religious, but scientific. Let's do it for ourselves. It's after all education."

"How can I leave my friend alone as we have decided to swim and sink together. Education never hurts as much as love." I claimed

"Why do you say that - fooled anymore, Pal?" I inquired.

"Because my cousin was duped for being less informed about astrology," I informed.

"Tell me what happened?" Pal asked curiously.

My cousin's marriage was getting delayed as per our society norms. Her mother was getting very anxious about the entire scenario. She was well educated and had her own business and was self-reliant. Yet, her mom's only aim was to get her daughter married sooner.

One day my aunt took her to an astrologer out of good faith, so they would know of the possible hurdles and act. The astrologer, after sensing my cousin's situation, and seeing her birth chart suggested she wear a ring with a particular stone. He insisted that the authentic stone could be bought from him only as he would specially bless the stone. He further instructed that the stone should be used in a ring made out of gold, and it should touch the index finger while wearing.

My cousin did everything as instructed because she admired her mom. She got the gold ring done with the stone mentioned purchased from the astrologer and wore the ring for six months. The proposals trickled in, but nothing spectacular or disastrous happened. One fine day, she decided to take off the ring. She observed the ring was not helping her in any way. Life was the same.

A year after taking off the ring, she happened to find it one fine day, and told her mom, 'Let's take this ring to the jeweller and I will make some other fancy ring in exchange.' The stone she purchased came at a considerable sum, and she asked the jeweller if he could buy it as he traded in stones. Her jeweller checked the stone and asked her, 'Where did you get it from? This stone seems artificial. You were duped.'

She had bad luck with both- the astrologer & the Jeweller - the first one duped her, and the second one gave her a shock.

She lost the colour of her face one instant, and another instant she was red with anger thinking how people make undue use of someone's situation.

"True," Pal affirmed, "Rather than aiding with a genuine service, they are here to misguide. Which in turn leads to more frustration and delayed results. No wonder, some people just give up on things after seeing no results."

"My cousin told her Mom not to take her to any astrologer henceforth for doing such rituals. My cousin eventually got married, despite not wearing crystals or stones. That episode and now this person calling you a Manglik," I remarked.

"I think, if I have to marry an authentic person, I have to learn astrology myself, so no one can fool me," Pal exclaimed.

"Let's master the skill," Pal suggested.

I too agreed, because although in my religion these practices don't matter, I am a science student, and I believe science behind them. When I believe in the planets and stars and their effect on earth, and so also us- humans.

Pal and I enrolled for an astrology course soon with a traditional astrologer and charted through the interesting insights we received all along.

Woah, we could read and interpret birth and astrological charts now. We also learnt about certain gems and stones and their significance in astrology.

"We are the *gyaanis* (well-informed) now!! Let's go save the world!" I proclaimed.

"True Pari. I'm not making this a hobby. I'm using this information as a life skill. Now, I know enough that no one can pull the wool over my eyes or push anything unnecessary on me. I now don't doubt the authenticity of these gemstones and recommended procedures, and at least know no one can deceive us," Pal uttered defensively.

I admitted that Pal had a point.

Chapter 8
The Mama's Boy

Pal mentioned another proposal had come through her maternal uncle. She explained that the meeting would be at the temple.

As we could not divulge Pal and my team and our motive, we agreed that Pal would fill me in on all the details afterwards.

Pal wasted no time and called me as soon as she got back home from the meeting.

"Hi, How was the meeting? Where were you dead all this while? I have been waiting for the last three hours to hear from you. I even texted you," I uttered excitedly.

"Not what I expected. When people ask stupid questions, I feel bound to be sarcastic and look for you." Pal answered dryly.

"Why, What happened?" I inquired.

"The guy seems to be very much in control of his parent's choice," Pal remarked.

"Spill the beans... I want to know it all. You have all my ears," I offered.

"His profile showed that his family is filthy rich. He had left his job and had ventured into a Hotel business. His father owned a restaurant, and his mother is a homemaker.

My initial expectation of this proposal was that the boy seems to be independent and ready to take on challenges. Getting into a business by leaving a stable job was not a cake walk. Although his family was in business, he too seemed to be thinking out-of-the-box and exploring a business for himself. He was not someone who wanted to follow the rat race in employment and wanted to do things his way. He seemed to have a vision for himself, and his life.

Looks interesting, thinking I asked my parents to set a meeting so we could meet and discuss face-to-face.

We met at our community temple as planned. The temple has a large prayer room where people could meet. I was initially awkward thinking about who meets in a temple for a matrimony meeting. There will be so many people out there praying that it would be difficult to talk freely.

My parents accompanied me to the meeting that was scheduled for 4.30 pm. We reached the temple on time. The boy's family walked in late.

It was past 5 pm when a huge car came into the temple premises. It was a new shiny silver SUV that seemed to be a latest buy. Its lustre and allure were enough to turn heads. The guy and his family walked out of it. My uncle mentioned, 'Oh here they are, finally.'

A lady, apparently the boy's mom, walked in front, followed by the boy, and a man in 50s, who seemed to be his father. The lady wore a designer saree and lots of artificial jewellery. The father seemed to be dressed flashily with 3-4 gold chains, gold bracelets and a couple of huge finger rings. The boy wore a white shirt and blue jeans with sports shoes. He wore a heavy gold chain around his neck, a huge bracelet around his wrist, and sported branded goggles. He reeked of perfume and seemed to be in his own world. He was balancing two cell phones in his hand. The cell phone covers appeared jazzy too.

As soon as the boy's mom approached us, she gave me a very exploratory look from top to bottom. I did not like the way she checked me. She made me feel that I was some display piece on sale. Although I had decided by now, I don't seem to be fitting as a part of such a flamboyant family, I decided to be further non-judgmental till I spoke to the guy. So, I forced myself to smile and greet them all.

As we settled in the prayer room adjacent to the temple, the boy's mom took the front seat and started showering me with questions. Both the men in their house took a back seat and remained mute. She started by asking- 'What's your education, your job. How much do you earn? Where do you spend all your salary or if you saved? Why did you graduate in this certain field only? Will you be working after marriage? We want someone who can work and earn. Do you cook? What is your specialty? We are all very fond of eating and although we run restaurants, our food is strictly prepared at home. We cook for ourselves. Do you do puja-pat? Do you know about our religious rituals? Do you know how to drape a saree? What is your Gotra?' And her interrogation went on.

I answered all her questions patiently, while fuming inside.

"Pal, you should have counter questioned her, after all you are also new to her family. You could have asked - Why do you have only one son? Why are the men in your house wearing more gold than the woman of the house? Will you continue cooking food if I marry your son because I will be at work? Why are you wearing a designer saree and not a traditional one in the temple? Why did you get your car inside the temple premises, and not park it outside? Why did you deliver a boy and not a girl?

Sometimes you need to give them the taste of their own medicine," I interrupted.

I wish you were with me Pari during all this, Pal chuckled and claimed, "I knew you would come up with something like this, I missed you there."

While I was answering the questions, I expected at least by now we could have some conversation and exchange information - however his mom was not giving him a chance to speak. I felt a bit disappointed by her behaviour. After 15 minutes of thoroughly scrutinizing, she told her son, "I have asked enough for now. You guys can talk now." She kept hovering around.

I was further bowled with her straight forwardness when she told me, "Listen, be mindful of what you ask my boy. Don't ask any unnecessary questions. I know today's generation girls are very smart and ask all unnecessary questions to the groom. They feel as if they can conquer the world with the way they think."

"Pal, You should have told her smilingly, aunty, I am already tired of answering your MCQs. And aunty, you are not from my generation, and you are still asking so many questions, so why can't I?" I chipped in.

"Pari, in fact, I did find her statements rude. If she had a daughter, I am sure she wouldn't be making such statements. After all she is also a woman, and she had kept her word without any request or fear.

What was she after all, a woman, right? How can she be so biased against another woman/girl? When I saw my mom's face, I knew she was disheartened by what the lady said. At that very moment I knew my parents had their answers ready, and they knew what my answer would be. Now it was just a formality." Pal shared.

"Pal, I think we decided to speak up for ourselves, and not take on anyone's undue bullshit. Haven't we?" I exclaimed

Pal replied, "I told her firmly, I want to speak to your son in person."

She was a bit surprised by my bold request and raised an eyebrow. She then looked at her son and signalled him to go along with me and sit in another corner of the prayer room. He clearly seemed uninterested to even initiate.

I had already made a decision to say NO. Especially after seeing his mom's attitude. Yet, I didn't want to be partial and thought of speaking to the guy once.

I started the conversation with the boy asking about his new business, his vision, and what his goal is in life. To my surprise he mentioned, 'I am doing this business only because dad has invested a lot of money. As it is, I was not happy at my previous job. I might as well sit at the restaurant counter and manage the business. Let me tell you, I don't have to worry about my future. My dad has made a lot of money for us and our next generation to survive comfortably.'

I could not help thinking- seems he has all the spoons in his mouth - silver, gold, platinum. How rich can one be?

I still persisted by asking, 'You may have some dreams or goals to achieve?'

He plainly retorted, 'I just want to spend money & live a lavish life. I am not concerned whether I am earning or not.'

He started adjusting the gold rings in his fingers. He was distracted, and kept flipping his phones, and checking them on and off.

I was a bit shocked hearing this. There was a battle of emotions running deep down in my heart. In the meantime, his phone beeped. He checked it and became restless. I asked him if he was alright and if he would like to ask me anything.

I was sure that it was his mom who messaged him.

He read it first, looked in the direction of his mom and then replied, 'See, all my decisions are made by my Mom, and it will be so in the future too. If she is ok, then I am fine too. She is the queen at home, and no one interferes with her decision. Right from where I am to what I do, I have to keep her informed all through the day.'

"The guy was like a bull wearing the bells because his horns didn't seem to work. Is it?" I asked as if I had decoded the guy and his personality already.

"You are right, Pari. He was now adjusting his gold chains round the neck, having kept his phone on his lap. As he moved, the phone fell down, and its glass broke. He suddenly exclaimed, Oh Shit, I need to order a similar custom piece now."

On checking it once I couldn't help saying, 'Seems it is only the tempered glass that has broken.'

He shared, 'Mom says we should not keep broken glass or pieces at home.'

'And for that you will take an entire new phone. You can even change the glass.' I suggested.

He did not reply. He was busy scrutinizing his phone as there was a message beep on his phone once again, and this time, he read the message and shifted in his chair. I then looked in the direction of his mom. She was looking at us. So, I asked him, 'Is everything alright?'

He explained, 'It's Mom, she wants to know if we are done talking.'

I offered, 'With pleasure. Since you have time constraints, we can end our talk here.'

I was now sure of my nudging intuition that told me NO already. There was no need to do any character match with this boy. He was the sure wrong one. I had made up my mind.

As soon as we returned back, his mom was standing and looking at us. Her stance and her expression were such that I had a very sinister feeling that she would bombard us with some statement. If this time she does, I will give it all back with a bonus, I thought.

I did not give her an opportunity to speak and told my parents we should leave now as we have to attend a function. My parents understood what I meant.

We were not interested in this proposal as we saw the boy was totally dominated by his mother. We decided this family is not meant for us.

After all, marriages are the union of families. Who raises a child like that - dependent? It makes me wonder about their parenthood. The boy has no sense of responsibility or individuality and is doing business unhappily just because his father has invested in it. How can his mom decide the compatibility for his partner? It is not a piece of garment or a house interior design that his mom can decide everything for him. The guy doesn't have his say in anything. His father too remained aloof and distanced."

"Here's another mother's son looking to marry. Why? Mumma's boys should not marry, they know they have the potential to ruin a girl's life. However, Moms are the most beautiful creatures on this planet, and there is no comparison to anything. They are the biggest shield, support anyone could ever have. I am not against any mom, yet, in this case, it feels like the guy isn't living his life and is a mere puppet, who has no control over his own life." I expressed.

"Most of all, I found his mother rude right from the beginning. I am afraid in the future there might be nasty differences between us." Pal exclaimed, "My dad has been a businessman all his life. I too was once from an affluent background. Even after losing his successful business to his own brother, my dad has been able to start from scratch and build another business shortly. I have seen his struggle.

He was a man who was affluent and went to zero and again earned a fortune for himself. Even after losing his business and money, my parents raised me in a very humble environment and taught me to respect others and the hard-earned money. He never showed off- No flashy cars, mobiles, or even jewellery. I think that's again an individual choice I don't want to judge someone on.

One thing is undeniable, today, what I am is all my parents' humble upbringing that keeps me down to earth and grounded, despite our financial status. Money should not get in your head, be it your own hard-earned money or your parents. The drive to work, to perform, to prove, to succeed should be inherent and not shrouded under your flashy materialistic toys."

"Pal, mothers are protective of their children. They do have an influence on the children in different ways. I cannot say if it's right or wrong. Although yes, this influence is very obvious.

I have a cousin who is very average-looking, very thin, and extremely unglamourous. She is of our age, and there came a time when her mother, my Dad's cousin, started looking for marriage proposals for her.

Now there came good proposals where she was often rejected. Her mother had trained her in how to sit, stand, walk, behave, dress, and talk when someone came to see her. It was like a performance that she had to put up with every time someone came to see her. Somehow, she was rejected by every guy.

Once when my Dad asked her mother how the matchmaking process is going, she admitted the scenario. My dad offered, for the next proposals, let's have the meeting at my house. My Mom got some dresses stitched for my cousin and would make her ready herself.

The difference was, my Mom told my cousin, 'Just be yourself when you are talking to the guy. While they ask you something, you can ask them questions too.' When it was time for my cousin to go and see the guy, she asked my Mom to pin her dupatta on her head. My mom asked, 'Why so?'

She answered, 'My mom always does that to me.'

My Mom asked her, 'How do you normally take the dupatta?'

She replied, 'Preferably around my neck. I am not used to dupatta on my head, and thus I am not confident.'

My Mom suggested, 'Then take the dupatta around your neck.'

She asked, 'Will it do? Will my mom be offended if I don't put a dupatta on my head?'

My Mom assured her, 'Yes. It's ok. Now go and be yourself. Just go and have a general conversation with the guy.'

That first meeting at our house was the day my cousin was herself, and the guy immediately gave his positive response. She liked the guy too, and soon they were married.

So, parents only think good for their children, and in doing that they have a certain influence. Now, it is up to the guy to decide what he is comfortable with."

Pal remarked, "I understand all that you say Pari. There is a distinction between being respectfully abiding and being totally controlled by parents. I had the latter feeling. Looks like whoever established the high roads needs to review it."

"Expectations are soupy noodles, slithery, and hard to control," I opined.

"Pal, there was a proposal for me, if you recollect me telling you. They had come to see me. When the guy's mom asked the guy to talk to me on a one-to-one basis, can you imagine, he went and asked his father, 'Can I talk to Parizad?'

Seriously, parental permission to talk to a prospect you are there to see. Do they ever take permission to stalk a girl, take a girl or date, or even to propose to her? Why are they now wearing a crown of sophistication and soberness? Frankly, I wouldn't have been so alarmed if he asked my parent's permission to talk to me, but his own father. Now that is what you are saying - totally controlled.

I was so surprised with this conduct that I told my family, 'After marriage, is he going to ask his father before coming to our bedroom too? Like, how kids ask the teacher, can I go to the toilet?'

Well, we all have respect for our parents, and should have. Yet, some decisions are our own. When you are in control of someone's expectations, you might end up hurting your other relationships." I mentioned.

"That is what I am scared of Pari," Pal expressed.

"Honey, don't ever date a mama's boy, she will always interfere in your business." I laughed and warned her.

"Hahaha, you are always right my angel, and hence I come to you." Pal mentioned.

"It is always easier to dump a mama's boy than divorce a mama's boy," I advised. "Our population is big enough to give you many choices. Don't you worry. The right one is just about somewhere in that crowd making his way to be seen."

"Yes, you won't believe there's another line-up by Mom," Pal announced.

"Omg, my dear friend is no less than a princess at her Swayam Var." I exclaimed.

Chapter 9
The Dominating Guy

Pal's mom made her sit beside her and explained, 'Pal, I have to discuss this proposal that has come through our neighbour.' Although Pal was not very keen about exploring the proposal, she knew she could not hurt her mother's feelings and accepted her request. Her Mom showed her the guy's picture on her old touch screen phone.

On a cursory glance based on his dressing and appearance, the guy appeared matured to Pal. Her Mom stated, 'The boy's family stays on the outskirts of our town and the guy has recently purchased his own big apartment near our house. He is a businessman and has his own office too. That's what any parent wants - a well settled guy.'

While Pal's Mom had her boxes ticked, all that crossed Pal's mind was, if this match happens, I will be near my parent's place. That was the only positive point she saw in this proposal. She did not think about his business, nor his possessions or even look for that matter.

She told mom, 'Let me meet him first, and then you get involved if it has to go any further.' After initial communication, Pal decided to meet the guy at our regular Cafe.

"Be ready tomorrow," Pal told me, "We are meeting the guy tomorrow at our cafe at 7 pm. I will be in the active mode, and you will be in stealth mode."

"Oh Wow! One more character!!" I exclaimed.

As discussed, I was to sit in her near vicinity and observe the guy and what he said. The cafe was mostly occupied by youngsters, and we were regulars here. This place was known to us and so were the staff.

We walked separately - Pal followed by me. When we reached there, the guy was already sitting at one of the corner tables overlooking huge windows and a good view. I was impressed by his punctuality. Well, one positive thing I must say in his favour.

Before I sat, I saw that he didn't even smile when Pal wished him 'Hi.' In fact, he didn't even reply to her pleasantries. He seemed to be a bit aloof.

I took a place behind the guy strategically so I could hear what they both said. In my mind, I was making my notes, recording every minute detail. After all, I was the bridesmaid on a special task- Mission Matchmaking.

Then Pal asked him, "Since when have you been here?"

He replied, "Just 10 minutes."

I wanted to see the guy's face. I stood up as if I was talking on the phone, standing near the human-sized window, twirling around, I had all eyes on him. The guy looked more mature than in his picture. There was a certain strain on his forehead, suggesting he was thinking a lot.

I observed his every move while pretending to talk on the phone. His dressing style, his mannerisms, his conduct, his approach. He wore a sky-blue shirt, with gray pants. The shirt was neatly tucked in under a black belt, and he looked presentable. He was continuously fidgeting with a phone in his hand. His phone's screen light was on, so I assumed he was on a call or nervously scrolling through his phone before we came. When Pal tried to call him before she walked into the cafe to ask where he was, his phone was busy, and he did not bother to call her back.

I was unsure about Pal's decision, although this guy would have to convince me first to marry Pal. I could see arrogance oozing through his various orifices.

I went and took my place, behind him, not to make my presence obvious.

He then filled the silence between them by saying, "I like Espresso, and so I have already ordered two Espressos for us."

Pal thought I am very Indian by taste, and black coffee is not my thing. I am more of a chai or a milk coffee person. Not every Indian would like the taste of black coffee at the first go.

"Oops, poor fellow, I thought, you missed one more mark here. You should always ask the lady what she wants, and not assume what she likes." I wondered.

My eyes seemed bigger than an ostrich's eggs. I sensed a little disappointment hearing this. He did not feel it was important to even ask Pal before placing an order.

Pal likes cappuccino, and the guy ordered Espresso. He could not wait for her to order or for that matter be courteous to ask her what she wanted to drink.

I came back and sat in my chair.

The silence between them was unhappening. I thought I was missing something, like suddenly my hearing aid was not working and a major crisis averting dialogue was being delivered.

Wait, I can't hear you guys. I fidgeted to hear clearly. I figured they were just silent.

I failed to tell my friend; a written questionnaire helps any day. We will be better prepared next time, Pal. For God's sake, for my sake, ask something. Anything.

I had the severe urge to turn around and ask the guy questions on behalf of Pal. I wondered what his reaction would be after knowing I am part of this matchmaking game. I held on to my horses.

Finally, like my hearing aids had miraculously got back their signal, I heard Pal's voice as she asked, "So what are your hobbies? Do you watch movies? I like watching movies & reading books."

He replied in an obviously satirical tone, "I run a business. I don't have time to watch movies - usually people who have a lot of time may waste time by watching movies. I work on weekends too, as it is my own business. That leaves me with little time for myself.

You must know that I and my team have almost cracked a major project, and we are projecting huge profits soon."

I clarified to him in my mind, "My team and I, is the right grammar, Sir. Or are you just being a boastful Narcissist?"

By the way, he just spoke ill about watching movies. He thinks it is a waste of time. Whereas Pal is a thorough movie freak.

Oh, my dear God! I want to hear how this is going to end. Although my back is towards them, I can very well sense Pal's anger must have risen like a sudden volcano about to erupt.

While I wanted to hear Pal's reaction and they were not pretty audible to me, I pulled my chair behind, and the table towards me making the screeching noise. For a moment, everyone looked in my direction while I turned to see the guy's reaction, and here we were looking into each other's faces.

I bit my tongue and blurted sorry for being noisy!!

Pal giggled.

While he talked to Pal, his phone continuously kept vibrating on the table.

Pal certainly seemed offended with his remark about movies, and said in response, "Good for you then. Nevertheless, one should take time for hobbies too - otherwise life will be too boring."

There was silence again after this conversation. I wished the guy was fluently silent at this particular time as it was the need of the hour.

Their coffee arrived and since it was our usual coffee shop, and the staff was acquainted with our orders, the staff looked at Pal and asked, "Mam how come you are having an Espresso today, you always have a Cappuccino."

She explained, "Yes, I planned to try something different today to give this gentleman company. On second thought it looks like I will require my regular cappuccino."

When the staff left, Pal told the guy, "I am not a black coffee person, and I can't even gulp it in." He did not reply, just started having his coffee. He seemed to be in a rush, and eager to go.

"Why didn't you tell me before?" He asked after some definite ruminating.

"You never asked me before," Pal acknowledged calmly.

I could sense the coldness in her voice and thought, first no greetings, then no consent and now no movies. This doesn't seem to be going anywhere.

Again, to cover the screaming silence Pal asked him, "What are your expectations from your partner? I want to keep working even after my marriage."

He instantly replied, "Why do you need to work? I am there to fulfil all your needs; I don't believe in girls earning their money. They earn peanuts but then have a lot of tantrums."

Pal asked him, "What makes you so opinionated about girls? People don't work only for money, they want to do something in their life, they have their dreams & goals to be achieved. I have my own identity. I too have my dreams and aspirations. My education and my potential are way beyond just doing household chores."

I could feel that Pal was now being restless and was chanting every possible prayer to stay calm, perhaps worrying that I would revolt back, or take her side against the guy.

Woah! What? I am unsure about Pal's decision. On the other hand, I strike him out here completely. Although, I thought, No, No, Honey! So far, I strike you off for Pal, and now I strike you off from marrying the entire womankind.

I could see Pal raising her eyebrows at his comment before saying anything further.

How could I! Pal and I had an agreement that I would always be the silent observer. Yet, if someone had this perception of a girl I would definitely turn around and start questioning him. Despite this, I contained myself.

I was so happy imagining it all that I snorted. People looked at me as my coffee oozed out of my nose. I was at the peak of embarrassment that I did not look around this time.

There was absolute silence after the guy heard what Pal said.

He then asked Pal if she could cook.

Pal answered, "Yes, I will not let anyone starve."

Here I chuckled, I knew Pal could cook bare minimum, and of course she will ensure no one goes hungry. She was not the chef kind or the girl next door who had a skill at cooking. She would definitely hold Darwin's title - Survival of the fittest.

The guy was in a rush. He did not ask any more questions once his coffee was over, and soon called for the bill. I was astonished at his behaviour.

Pal did not stop him from leaving, if he must. Good that he decided to leave, or else I would have pledged my promise and answered him back before Pal could.

When the bill came - to my surprise - he started arguing with the staff about the bill amount, as it had an additional tax included in the main amount. He told the staff, "You are fooling people."

The staff explained, "Sir, this amount was already mentioned in the menu & the surcharge & taxes are included overall everywhere. How can we fool you?"

I could see Pal felt a bit embarrassed. She must be thinking, it seems like this man is coming out of his kingdom for the first time. Looks like he isn't aware of the GST and other charges in the bill. In fact, she was angry at him - the way he was treating people. Sometime back he was blabbering about his projects & profits and here he was arguing with this staff for such a trivial amount.

Pal offered to him, "No problem, this bill is on me as you came here in this cafe on my request."

He argued, "No, you don't have to pay. I will pay the bill. Anyways when we meet next time for lunch or dinner, that time we will see. There is a good Chinese restaurant near my workplace, we can meet there."

I couldn't stop thinking about how overconfident he was that Pal will meet him again, where she must have already rejected him in her mind. If he knew how to decode body language, he could have obviously seen this.

I read Pal's mind, "Does he think he has made a good impression on me? I am not a fool to meet you again?"

He continued, "I presume, you will say yes to your family for my proposal??"

Pal was caught in a situation now and she flinged back in a calm and polite manner, "I don't think. I take it the other way. I won't be comfortable meeting you again. Our wavelengths do not match. We hardly spoke anything. I am assuming we would not explore anything differently in the next meeting."

I wanted to see his reaction now, and I again pretended to be on the phone near the glass window having his full view.

I saw his face and expressions were changing to her reply. His face had beads of sweat, his skin appeared red hot, and I could see him flaring his nostrils already.

He asked, trying to keep his voice in control, "Why would you deny me? You hardly know me."

Pal was getting a lot more irritated with his statements and retorted, "What's the use of saying Yes, when we both have a different perspective of looking at life and especially your way of seeing a woman."

He then insisted, "I don't want to hear anything - just say Yes. Things will turn out to be in your favour later on. You will see. I am a well settled businessman. You don't have to worry about your financial needs." He was very adamant.

Pal was furious now and replied, "I do not wish to get married to someone who holds such an opinion about women and how they work and earn. I do not know what peanut money is, but for a few of them- it's their money, their income, their livelihood, with which they run their families. Any money earned is valuable."

The guy left stating, "So that's it then!!"

I joined Pal at her table soon after the guy left.

We went together to Pal's home. Pal's mom was waiting for her and was expecting everything to have gone well. She was basically expecting a positive answer from Pal. In fact, the guy's parents had already called Pal's parents and communicated their 'Yes.'

Pal told her parents what happened in the evening and also gave her objection to the proposal.

Pal told her mom, "He is all against the way you have brought me up. He has a different set of mentality for working women and wants to have things his way. He thinks women should just follow men, and he did not even bother to ask about my decision - even for a coffee. He assumed my answer to be yes, despite me telling him about our differences. I don't think I can get along with him."

Pal's Mom agreed with Pal and mentioned that I will convey your reply to them.

When Pal's Mom called the guy's Mom and conveyed her reply. The guy's Mom was agitated and stated, 'We said yes in the very first meeting. Your daughter does not understand the worth of my son's proposal. He is well settled and independent. Your daughter, despite being arrogant, my son has chosen her. You don't know how she answered my son when he asked, 'Can you cook food?' She could say Yes, but she responded, 'I will not let anyone starve.' Despite all this we have replied with a Yes. Make some sense to your daughter.'

Pal's Mom calmly clarified, 'I know my daughter and she cannot be arrogant, and however, her decision is my decision. I have taught her self-respect and that men should know to respect a woman, regardless of cooking or no cooking, earning or not earning. If she is not doing this, she is not invalid. She is not less of a woman.'

Back in her room Pal shared, "My parents have raised me in an open and independent environment where I have the freedom of speech and expression. Whatever the issues or challenges at home, my parents always discussed them openly, and often I was a part of the discussion, where my opinion was also considered.

Raised in such an environment when because of marriage, your partner would want you to stop working, and depend on them totally, it seemed like a red signal for me. Being dependent on money would eventually stretch the dependability for decision too on the partner. Although I am well educated and make a decent living, the position and respect I have earned for myself as a professional is more important to me than living a life fostering my partner's priorities and career, while giving up mine.

Every girl today has a career, and if she wishes to maintain her career post marriage, I feel it is not selfish. Rather, if she finds her professional and personal growth happening alongside her partner, she will be much happier to contribute to that relationship."

"One word for it all, I already REJECTED the guy for you Pal. I know you so well." I concluded.

Chapter 10
The Arrogant Guy

A couple of days later, Pal called me and declared, "Time to go on another quest. There's a new proposal, and I have to meet him today. Are you game?"

"I can be good company when there is good coffee," I offered, and we laughed.

"By the way, where are we seeing the guy?" I asked.

"Our cafe it is!!" Pal mentioned.

"The guy's profile is not very impressive, but I did not trust what people write on their profile anymore. I wanted to meet him and know more about him.

He has stated that he was well-settled Deputy Manager and lived with his parents, and that he is the only child." Pal apprised me.

Like last time, we split just before entering the cafe. Luckily, we were seated at two adjacent tables. I carried my laptop to pretend I was working. The guy was late, and so we could settle.

When I saw him, I found him charming and very stylish. The way he dressed, he looked prim and attractive.

On the other hand, Pal was a simpleton, and I am sure she must have assumed the guy would have high expectations for his wife. Definitely someone extremely attractive, and much complementing his physical charm.

Pal was of the opinion, not every encounter could be fruitful or lead to marriage, some people could remain acquaintances or even become good friends for life.

The meeting was a good one. Both Pal and the guy were either smiling or laughing. Here's something cooking, I thought. I am sure, something good. I could not hear much this time, as it was noisy around.

"He said, let's keep in touch," Pal told me once the guy left. "He seems to be good looking and good at talking as well and I found myself talking to him effortlessly."

In addition, Pal and he talked every day on the phone, and their messaging continued throughout the day beyond the regular good morning and good night. From hobbies to interests, food and travel, movies, and cafes, they also explored the fancy of being husband and wife someday.

Over time, he didn't send Pal any messages for two days at a stretch and she found it strange and called me. Pal was concerned now, hoping that everything was okay. She had one such ghosting experience in the past and was nervous.

I told her, "Just call him up. You guys talk often. He must be busy with something. Why bother over a trivial thing."

Pal called him to ask about his day, and he didn't answer. The next day, the same thing happened. A whole week passed, and Pal did not hear from the guy. She was sure by now that something was wrong.

Despite calling him and texting him, he didn't respond. Pal was clueless if something was really wrong with him, or he too was suddenly ghosting on her.

"Do I stop texting and calling him? His not answering is a sign that maybe he doesn't want to talk to me, or genuinely something is wrong." Pal asked me concerned.

Pal was incubating her thoughts before even verifying them in the absence of any communication.

"Does he have an identity crisis? Like square box, round pizza, and triangle slices?" I asked.

"I saw his pics on social media and that is when it hit me, that he is avoiding me. I had forgotten that I had added him as a friend. To your dismay, I saw that he had been out partying with friends and colleagues for the last couple of days. I don't mean he should not party. However, he should at least communicate," Pal uttered agitatedly, "I am not angry, just confused. I couldn't believe that he was out having fun, while I was worrying about him. At this point, I told my parents everything that had happened, just so that they do not keep any hope in us. My parents have been supportive and understanding. They told me that it was normal to feel this way, and that I should call him again one last time before I end it all."

Pal continued, "I am sure now I don't want to call him. I don't want to be ignored again, just like the previous calls and messages that went unanswered."

Next day Pal mentioned to me, "Just to conclude this, last night, I sent him a message asking, Hello. Can you talk?"

He replied, 'I am busy with calls, and can only chat.'

I calmly asked, 'You can continue to be busy. I just wanted to check on you if you are ok. I tried calling and messaging you many times.'

He mentioned, 'I have been busy with work. I have been feeling very overwhelmed and stressed.'

I told him, 'It is ok to have your space. Ideally you should have at least communicated with me. I have been writing and calling you.'

He was infuriated reading my message, and reacted, 'I think you are trying to get attached to me too soon. We have just met. It's common sense to know that if I wasn't replying, I must be busy or did not want to be disturbed.'

I was taken aback reading his reply. For a moment I thought someone else was texting from his phone. The person who has been conversing with me so lovingly is now rude to me.

I asked him, 'I couldn't know what was going on in your life and nor did you tell me. I would have appreciated it if you had left me a message saying, DO NOT Disturb. I would have happily left you in your space.'

He replied, 'That is the problem with you girls, you need to be informed of everything, and don't have common sense or patience to wait. Especially, why are you behaving like a middle-class girl?'

I couldn't believe that he would say something like that to me especially after showing such care and understanding initially. I was in shock and disbelief. I told him, 'Firstly, I sent you a message because I was concerned about your well-being. It's a human tendency to check if someone disappears suddenly. Last but not least, if caring for someone is middle class in your dictionary, then I am a middle-class girl. You make me ponder about your class now. I definitely do not want to fall into your class category where people are so inhuman. I would like to leave you in your space, and won't message you any further, not even as an acquaintance. Have fun with your class.'

Pal had her fangs out and asked me, "Pari, what do you think is middle-class? How can we classify someone so?"

I asserted, "Sad, yet true, a fraternity in our society is termed as middle class. It is slang - the middle class is considered a personality, which is considered unambitious and just running after their daily earnings, no dream, no goal, no fortune, or any financial backup."

Pal said, "First, he classified me as a Middle class good for nothing girl. I think any person who earns and struggles for a living, be it any class, deserves respect. They are not fortune hunters, just making ends meet, or growing in their professional life at their pace.

To understand the difference of each other's time, profession and expectations is humanity. To empathize and not classify is humanity. To show interest and be true to your emotion even when the interest has faded and communicate right is humanity.

I saw this guy lacked basic humanity.

The second thing that struck me hard was he was assuming I was being possessive about him, which was not the case. I have a moral upbringing and for me it's important to have my space, as I might give anyone theirs. As girls, women we are wired differently, we tend to be emotionally attached, and care more as compared to guys and men. This is how we are built naturally, and this is how we behave. Considering my natural instincts as possessiveness was like blaming me for entering his personal space uninvited.

However, it's good that some things happen early in time. It was a wakeup call to be less expecting of people."

"Pal, I want to give a standing ovation to this guy with my tallest finger." I announced.

Pal's mood immediately lit up, and we got back to our usual banter.

Chapter 11
The Confused Guy

Pal's friend set this proposal for her. Despite the age difference of seven years, Pal decided to give it a chance and meet the person. The guy's biodata looked decent. Although it was very average to my liking. He had an average height, average in academics, average salary, and average looks.

Pal expressed, "I do not want these to be the mere criterion to reject him at such a preliminary stage. I would like to consider someone for their merits and qualities rather than making assumptions solely based on age."

"He is 7 years younger than you," I reminded.

"The 7- year gap although is nagging me, I am willing to look beyond the age factor and see if there were positive qualities or aspects in the person that I could appreciate. People from different age groups often bring diverse life experiences, wisdom, and insights. By being open to this meeting, I am hoping to discover some shared interests, common values, or simply enjoy a meaningful conversation with someone who has a different perspective on life.

I had so far met many guys for marriage, might as well meet him, and who knows, he might be the one for me. Sometimes it's important to trust your instincts." Pal justified.

Pal decided to meet the guy at our usual café. I could not accompany her due to some work at hand.

Pal mentioned to me that evening, "He turned out to be a warm, and talkative person as opposed to my inhibitions. Sooner, we got to talking about the future that would be, and the topics around career and family. We found a lot of common stuff through our hobbies and likes.

However, one peculiar thing I observed about him was, he took ages to decide what he wanted to eat. He was swinging from one option to another. I let him decide, thinking maybe it was his first visit to this cafe and he is taking time while I was a regular there and I knew the menu like the back of my hand.

We spent a good one hour together and decided to meet again. Perhaps the next time more focused on the reason we were meeting for, and to delve deeper into each other's personalities, interests, and perspectives."

"Did you like him so much to have a second meeting?" I questioned.

"The decision to meet again is to give one more opportunity to understand each other and to be sure about our compatibility and potential for a future together even before involving our families." Pal admitted.

She shared, "We met in a mall, and the atmosphere was different as compared to the café."

He mentioned, "I want to buy a formal shirt, can we go check one?" I agreed. In the next two hours, we visited all the men's clothing shops in the mall, however he was unable to decide on one shirt. Colour, fitting, pattern, size, price and all the other reasons he had, to not pick one shirt.

We finally went and sat in the food court. This time too he was choosy, and finally ordered something after screening the menu for a good 30 minutes. My order was already there, and I ate before. As I was eating, he disclosed, "I know I take time to decide things. You must wonder, I have not even communicated my reply to you about what I feel about us."

I told him, "I am in no hurry to get married. Just that we are in an arranged marriage setup, and here weddings are arranged by seasons and availability of halls. Yet, I want to decide sooner and commit, because I do not want to get emotionally involved and eventually see the proposal not materializing. I hope you understand my point."

"Pari, with our meetings and intermittent conversations, I had somehow made up my mind to go ahead with this proposal. All the apprehensions of age, and averageness were blurred in the act of knowing him. Although, I did not want to pressurize him to make a decision; mine has been made. I am looking for a healthy and sustainable partnership and not just the traditional marriage bonding." Pal expressed.

"Dating a younger guy is good; after all they will never grow older than you," saying I tried to elevate Pal's mood.

"When I reached home, my parents questioned me about the guy's decision. After all, it was our second meeting. I could wait, however my parents might not. Culturally, they were accustomed to the norm that more than one meeting meant it was moving to something positive. They were more experienced and informed in these cases to see that I do not get emotionally attached to someone who might not pursue the relationship ahead. I knew my parent's concern, and I told them the fact that, 'He needs more time to think. He is still indecisive.'

My parents did communicate their discomfort on this. They weren't restless, they were being practical." Pal mentioned.

Pal called me the following weekend saying, "The guy asked me out again. I had already set clear boundaries for myself, no meeting the guy more than twice if they have not communicated their decision.

I called him and made clear that it would be difficult for me to meet and told him of my apprehensions as he is still undecided. After all, it was an arranged marriage and I was not dating someone, and he said, that's what he wants to meet and finalize."

"Go win the fort," I encouraged Pal.

Pal suggested, "I was expecting this would at least conclude somehow."

"Pari, do you wish to come and be my moral support? We are going to meet over dinner." Pal asked.

"Of course," I affirmed.

We met at a cozy quiet restaurant this time, a fine dine setup. Through an internal setting, I managed to book the tables behind them, so I do not miss out on anything.

The guy had dressed up in beige trousers and a maroon shirt. He sat on the chair first- oh boy how could you do this, I thought. Then suddenly he realized he should pull the chair for Pal. So, he stood up and pulled the chair for her. He then went back and sat on his chair.

Soon Pal was ready with her order, and this gentleman was still flipping a menu with 2 pages - 4 sides for a couple of minutes. I heard pal helping him to pick one by asking him questions about how hungry he is; accordingly, they could place an order.

"Oh, baby boy!" I thought, "Pal, stop being his Mom."

For me, sitting at the table all alone, I was wondering what I should order. I am the one who barely eats. Finally, I placed an order for a Quinoa salad. A pure non-vegetarian acting vegan. I also told them, get it as late as possible, maybe after 15-20 minutes. I have all the time.

There was too much noise in the restaurant with people chattering and the background music. Initially I could hardly hear them. As the crowd became scarce, they were audible to me.

He spoke about all the things, except his decision to marry. Towards the end of the meeting, Pal asked him, "I do not want to force you into a decision, although that's what our agenda was about meeting today. What have you thought about marriage?"

He claimed, "Look Pal, even when taking my official decisions, I take a lot of time, and this is my life. How can I be so sure in just three meetings?"

All that went in my mind was, "How is he still sustaining at work with this pace of decision making? Or maybe he is in some menial job where there is no decision making involved and he is claiming to be someone else. All these days I was observing his decision-making skills, nevertheless, he just confronted his weakness."

Pal subtly replied, "Sorry I can't go ahead with someone who is unable to decide. For me, If I want you, I want you. There is no second thought. I wish you the best with your future matchmaking endeavours," saying Pal left from there.

"Let me not bother him anymore - I don't want to spend my life with a guy who lacks decision making skills. Sometimes some decisions cannot be prolonged, or we have lost opportunities." Pal said, as we met outside the restaurant.

"I had made my flag ready to unfurl. I thought this time we are certainly celebrating our win," I blabbered.

Pal looked gloomy. I asked her, "What's bothering you?"

She expressed, "This arranged marriage system in itself is intimidating."

I asked, "What makes you feel love marriage is less intimidating? I think being confused is not wrong. Being so confused that you cannot decide on time might cost you some good opportunities. Like orange being - a fruit and a colour, and you don't know where to use what."

Pal replied, "When this guy was taking ample time to decide, I was focused on not being emotionally involved. After all, it was an arranged marriage set-up and there was no commitment to marriage. I was wary of such an engagement, and thus I insisted on a decision sooner.

Marriage is about two people. Your compatibility should be with your partner. Are both parties aligned in different aspects is something that needs to be ascertained. Families are important, however, they come later."

I exclaimed, "Sooner is an understatement. Although, my family was concerned and wanted me to meet new people and explore the possibility of remarriage. Over everything, they were concerned about my mental health, and they wanted me to start rethinking.

Divorce happened when I was told I was wrong at every single thing I did, and it was no longer working for me this way. You have spoken to 10 men by now, if I would have spoken to these many men, Adein would have divorced me 10 times.

Ironically, after my divorce I became vocal about how I felt."

I thought, while I am the expressive one, Pal is not so expressive. Although she conveyed what she felt to her parents, and seldom to the guys she met. We were hit with a plateau now. However, it was not over yet.

Chapter 12
Clairvoyance

I moved to Australia for my PhD. Pal and I were again physically distant. This time we knew we would be in touch. We were not little girls any more dependent on our parents.

Once I moved to Australia, the once continuous visions of my Beach Guy started coming to me again. In my dreams, he kept telling me he was coming to me, and he is on the way.

Although, our hot topic of discussion was Pal's marriage. While meditating I would get visions about how Pal's marriage would be. Pal and I often discussed the visions we had. We meditated together irrespective of time zones and place and often dwelled in our cumulative energies. We know we are always better together than facing something alone.

In my meditation, I got detailed glimpses of her guy. He was tall, well built, and maintained a good physique. I could see his background - that he is a fitness freak and enjoys gymming. He was a god - fearing person, and self-made.

He also had a prominent tattoo on his right arm. I could see it was the tattoo of Shiva. The beautiful intricate tattoo had a trident in his hand which had an artistic design. It was a huge tattoo which also spread to the back of his shoulder. The face of Shiva was complacent, kind of suggesting everything would be just fine.

I was so very excited to tell all this to Pal that I didn't wait to see what time it was and where she would be doing what.

I called her in the middle of the night and announced excitedly, "Pal, I saw his vision."

"Who's vision? It's late at night here. It must be later at your place. Haven't you slept yet?" Pal asked.

"Who cares. Shut up and listen to me. He is tall, smart, and has a good physique. He goes gymming regularly and is a fitness freak." I blurted.

"Ok babes let's start from the beginning. Who are you talking about? Your guy or my guy?" Pal asked.

"Your to-be-husband," I clarified.

Pal was quiet for a while on the call. I checked, "Are you here or reached the seventh sky already?"

"Did you seriously see him?" Pal asked curious.

"I had glimpses of him in my meditation. I saw him. He is the one for you. I could not have a clear vision of his face though. I also saw you guys getting married in a typical South Indian marriage."

"How do we differentiate this person? These days most guys go gymming," Pal asked.

I chipped in, "Tattoo my baby tattoo."

"Then again tattoos are so common today. How do we know who is the one?" Pal asked.

"True, we can't tell the guy to take his shirt off. Rather, we need to come up with some idea to get his shirt off to see the Shiva tattoo," I answered.

"Mission - Tattoo Guy begins!!" I declared.

Pal kept meeting the guys. Of course, now, with the newfound vision she got from me. She knew my dreams and my glimpses came true and was very hopeful.

How to get a guy's shirt off to check his tattoo, if any, was something Pal was dealing with now. The only thing on her mind was, what if the guy thinks she was physically craving?

Chapter 13
The Half-Truth Guy

The guy's credentials appeared to be very decent. His parents were retired, and he stayed with them. They were government officials. The guy was settled in a good job with a very handsome salary and worked in an IT company as a Manager. They lived in the Mumbai suburbs and had their own place. The guy had a younger brother too, who apparently was not staying with them.

Although now all these credentials don't matter to us. Our main focus was to find if the guy has a Shiva tattoo. Pal decided to meet this guy at our regular matrimonial cafe.

Pal called me to say, "I met this guy. He was dressed in casual attire, jeans and a half-sleeved t-shirt with sport shoes. He was tall, well built and had a good personality. Although he looked charming, his t-shirt was very vibrant and tucked out. He seemed to be too casual.

He asked what I wished to eat before we started a proper conversation. I settled for a sandwich and coffee, and he ordered a Pizza slice. We started conversing as we waited for our order. First about our parents, then about work. I told him I wish to keep working even after marriage and he stated, 'Why not!! Even my mother worked all her life. She has been a Research Scientist. Every girl, woman should be independent.'

We discussed our passion & work. I asked him about his hobbies, and he stated, 'Nothing much. I am so engrossed in software development that only the codes keep running in my head.'

I was interested in knowing if he has any tattoos. He was wearing a t-shirt, and his arms were clearly visible, and there was no tattoo on his arm. I knew he was not my soulmate. Pari's vision cannot be wrong. Since I was here to meet, I sat back.

We got into more discussions.

He told me, 'I am the eldest son, and I have a younger brother. While my brother stays separate, I have decided to stay back with my parents. They are retired and growing older.' He seemed to be a decent family-centric man, who respects his parents, and was willing to stay around to fulfil his duty as a son.

Our conversation went very smoothly, and we discussed movies, travel, books, outdoors and many more topics. I was waiting for the moment when he would give me some hint on why he is not the perfect guy for me.

Somehow, I was aware, and mentally prepared that something was not so right. There was a sudden silence between us, and just to fill in the silence, I asked him out of curiosity, 'Do you like kids?'

He promptly replied, 'I love kids. My younger brother's child is very naughty, and I love to spend time with him. He is just 3 years old, and an adorable chap.'

On this statement, something struck me. Wait a minute. He is the eldest son, and technically society wants the marriage to take place in chronological order, and so I asked him, 'You are the eldest son of your family, and your younger brother is already married and has a kid too. He got married before you? That's absolutely alright, but I am just curious how you are dealing with society?'

There was a sinister silence this time as if he were tongue-tied, and I wondered if I asked something I was not supposed to. Yes, it gave me that feeling.

In the meantime, he gathered himself and uttered, 'Actually, I am a divorcee, and I was married for seven long years. I got divorced last year. We separated amicably, and I was just about to tell you all this.'

I was stunned hearing this. There was a blur around me, like I was dizzy with this shocking revelation. I wasn't expecting this. He just gave me the reason why he is not my soulmate.

Trying to come back to senses, I mustered my strength and said – 'I wasn't aware of your background. Why did you keep this information a secret in the first place?'

He disclosed, 'I was married to the love of my life. However, after marriage things did not go well and we had to part ways. I had given her all the freedom. We were good friends before we married. We spent a good seven years together. Eventually, she needed more from the relationship which I could not provide. I will not ridicule any one of us here. I respect our decision, and we mutually separated.'

He continued, 'I thought after I meet you, I can make you understand. I really liked your profile, and I got very positive information about you. In fact, I have liked you and want to go ahead if you are ready to accept me. I can explain everything to you in detail.'

This moment was when I had to reply back to him. I looked at him and replied, 'I feel misinformed, and I can never believe such a person any further. I am not sure if I want to go ahead.'

I was flushed with emotions. I felt weak in the knees although I had given my answer. I left without allowing him to explain. It did not matter anymore.

I went home and narrated the entire thing to my parents who were equally dejected, firstly having misinterpreted the proposal, and now knowing the facts. My parents were surprised how his parents could hide the entire details.

My dad patted my shoulder and concluded, 'This is not the end of life. Don't be demotivated.'

We rejected the proposal."

Pal after much thinking asked me now, "Pari, you think it is right to hide things from people in such situations? My father had taught me the importance of open communication. Mind you, that does not mean one has to be straightforward, instead, be sensitive about what has to be spoken, where necessary. Time is the essence. As in this case, the guy was a divorcee and only after I came to know from his talks about his marital status and confronted him, did he respond that he was just about to tell me."

"Pal, I feel this is a totally subjective choice. Some may reveal, some might not. Some take time to say things when they are comfortable. Not everyone is particular about communicating everything in the first meeting," I mentioned.

"Don't you think it is a breach of trust in that case? Being a divorcee is not wrong, it's not a sin, and perhaps I would have looked at the guy with a different perspective. He was a nice proposal and eventually he resorted to giving justification when I confronted him with his own half-truth. If not for his profile, he would have at least told me of his marital status on the phone, or initiated the topic when we met," suggested Pal.

"Pal, you know I am a divorcee, and I do not openly go and claim to people that I am a divorcee. I have seen the wrong side of it. I have received ulterior and cheap messages from men when they learnt about my marital status, right from physical obligations to one-night stands.

One thing is clear, people do not let you stay alone in peace. The moment they come to know you are a divorcee. You are evaluated and judged - She only must be the problem. You are often asked questions that you cannot reply to openly in public. You are put through awkward situations because you are alone. You are made to feel that everything in your life is over now, and if you have to do something better in your life, accept the unacceptable to you. Because how else can you survive alone? I was asked for one-night stands, and I wanted to punch their nose. I was waiting for an opportunity to give it back to them and I did.

Remember, the battle is with you- yourself first, and then society.

In this case, I feel he should have at least given you a heads up about his marital status. Before going to meet a guy, I would have done it," I explained.

"Pari, I am not against him being a divorcee, I am against him telling me the half-truth. What you said is also right, the way people look at a divorcee, and how they treat one. At least when you meet guys, they know your marital status. You are prepared, and the reason you are not accepting them is because of your past. That's a different issue. If he had told me earlier, or mentioned in the biodata, I would have been prepared accordingly.

I discovered his half-truth before he could confide in me. This does not apply only for the divorcee status, perhaps for many other things in a relationship. Saying things at the right time is crucial.

Nevertheless, he was not my soulmate. I identified it in the beginning when I could not see a tattoo on his arm. I was focused. I only wanted to see how after coming across so perfect, he is not my guy. I got my answers." Pal replied.

"Good we did not go to the extent of making him remove his shirt to check his tattoo," I concluded, and we laughed.

Chapter 14
The Gold Digger

"Pari, a friend wants to introduce me to this guy claiming this guy harbours a secret crush on me. I was piqued with curiosity. Intrigued, I agreed to meet him after many requests, albeit with the clear understanding that I was on a quest for a lifelong commitment, not a fleeting romance.

All I thought was, what if this guy had a tattoo on him." Pal expressed.

"And then? Fill me in with the details girl, common," I replied.

Pal started, "When we met, I did recollect seeing him at a common friend's get together. When we started talking, it was like we already knew each other. Our conversations flowed effortlessly, and our shared interests created a bridge between our different worlds. I asked him all the questions parked in my mind, hinting to make him disclose why and since when he had a secret crush on me.

I did not see it in his eyes. I did not feel it in his talks. I could only sense that he was being a nice person, and there was nothing beyond that. I was grappling with the uncertainty of his feelings as my friend had mentioned to me.

We did meet and spoke over calls casually. Over our meetings, I tried to find if he had any tattoos on him. Although he did not look like he would get a tattoo. Yet, I couldn't be judgmental. During one of our conversations, I slipped into a question about tattoos. He exclaimed surprised, 'Tattoo and me? Why do you think I could get a tattoo? Do you like it?'

This puzzled me. Maybe my judgment was right that he can't have a tattoo.

When he saw the puzzled expression on my face, he laughed out loud and responded, 'I was teasing you. Of course, I have a tattoo.' He pulled his shirt sleeve up and there on his wrist was a small horizontal tattoo that read the signs of Rupee, Dollar, Euro, and Pound.

Oh, this is not the Shiva tattoo Pari mentioned about. I thought.

I asked him, 'What does this mean?'

He replied, 'It's a reminder that money is important in one's life, then it could be in any colour or symbol,' and smiled.

Pal asked, 'Do you have any other tattoo other than this?'

He expressed, 'No, this is the only one, the only important thing in a man's life - Money.'

Between casual talks, he expressed his desire to be in a relationship with me. This was a face-off moment. I did not want to spoil things and appear curt, and hence replied calmly, 'I am looking for a life partner and not a boyfriend.'

He used some charming words that could easily make someone fall for him. I found it silly and a bit foolish.

I replied cautiously, 'You are amazing. You have become like an all-season buddy.'

In the next two days we met again for coffee after work. This time he claimed, 'I spoke to my parents. They are ready to accept you as their daughter-in-law. There is just one small condition.'

Not that I was keen on marrying him, however he made me curious, and I asked, 'What condition?'

According to Pari's vision, I knew that he was not the guy for me, yet as a human tendency and as friends I wanted to understand what the condition was.

My Mom says, 'You can marry a girl of your choice. My only expectation is 50 tolas of gold from the girl's family for marriage. After all, I am their only son, and this is her condition to whoever marries me.'

I screamed, '50 tolas (20 ounces)!! Are you even in your senses? Are you playing a prank on me?'

He replied complacently, 'Why prank, giving gold in marriages is still a common practice in our society?' He appeared very serious as he stated this.

I was shocked and blatantly replied, 'Oh, so you are on sale, and your price is 50 tolas gold. Hmm!! Your parents must think you are too worthy to ask that amount.'

He tried clarifying, 'Pal, I want you to know that I am personally against dowry. It goes against my principles.'

'I'd agree with you, but then we'd both be wrong,' I stated.

He hesitated for a moment before responding, 'By the way, it's for the bride. She will only be the one wearing it.'

'What if the bride doesn't want to wear gold, silver, diamonds, or fancy things. Now what?' I asked with a raised voice.

Knowing my reaction, he looked deep into my eyes, and replied with a hesitation, 'If you are ready, I can negotiate and get it down to 25 tolas. I know it's a compromise, although at least that much obligation is required.'

I nodded with my eyes wide like an owl, my mind grappling with my anti-dowry principles. I wondered if I should yell at him or be calm. Till some time back I perceived it all as love and now it had gotten down to business negotiation.

He asked, 'Why are you silent?' His tone was tinged with a hint of frustration. 'It's common in a marriage to ask for gold. If it's not your family, it would have been someone else's.'

I looked at him and thought, didn't you decode the look on my face? It just says SHUTUP!

'Good for you. You are on sale and that too negotiable. Go find some other customers. I am not here to buy a husband.' I replied sarcastically.

Now his tattoo made complete sense to me and so did his approach to money. Looks like he loves the wealth I have, and thus built up this crush story. Maybe there was never a crush or emotion in the first place. My anger was at the next level. However, I didn't want to lose my temper, and at the same time wanted to put across what I thought was right. If not me, then he will play the same crush card with another girl.

I took a deep breath, and with a calm and clear tone exclaimed, '50 tolas! That's a fortune!! Frankly, I think it would be better if you could find another family that aligns with your family's demands. I'm not interested in entering into a family that places such materialistic expectations without even meeting me and knowing me for the person I am. Nor am I interested in marrying you for gold. I hope your family knows that asking for dowry is a crime.

I warn you not to do any such act in the future, or else you would land in trouble. I can easily put you behind bars. Nevertheless, I want to give you one chance, because we have been good friends. Change your and your family's mindset before it's too late.'

With those words, I uttered a decisive goodbye, marking the end of our journey together. I told him, 'Please do inform your mother, now after hearing all this I will not even keep you in my friend zone, forget Dowry!! I am glad to tell you, my answer to your proposal is a DEFINITE NO.'

As I walked away, a mix of emotions lingered in the air—relief, sadness, and a tinge of disappointment. I was determined to uphold my values and unwilling to compromise on my principles. After all, I was not here to buy a husband, perhaps win one for his qualities.

The prospect of his family's expectations, particularly the demand for gold, left me feeling distraught. The idea of an uncertain future, where his family might still be dissatisfied even after the marriage, haunted me. I couldn't shake off the worry about how any girl's parents would manage such demands.

However, I was satisfied that I made a point on behalf of the girl fraternity that taking dowry is a crime."

"Stay composed Pal." Pari mentioned as she heard it all. "He is just one of a kind. You have met the other specimens too. Seems pedigree is far from reality, and only in expectations now." I responded.

"Pari, the biggest joke is the guy who claimed to love me so much, has asked 50 tolas of gold from me, so he can marry me. Can you imagine I have to buy a husband now." Pal exclaimed furiously.

"Can he himself afford to buy 50 tolas gold? I don't think he can, or he would have not demanded it. I am shocked to hear that people demand dowry even after being educated and despite there being strict laws!!" I mentioned.

"Yes 50 Tolas, and this husband is negotiable, he has brought down his rate to 25 tolas after which there cannot be any further negotiation," Pal declared sarcastically.

"What about the love he claimed for you?" I am unable to stop laughing now.

A smile broke on Pal's lips, the creases on her forehead relaxed, she felt a change in energy with my laughter as she stated, "What love? He was investing in me emotionally so I could not deny him dowry. He wanted to be sure I was ensnared in his love that I would succumb to his demands. He just wanted to show off to his people that my wife is super rich, so he could impress them. Why does he want to show off my money, and to whom? He can't afford it, and I don't like to wear this much gold, so why the dowry?" Pal asked intrigued.

"We're really lucky that our parents support us and give us strength. Many girls can't even speak up or stand up for themselves against this unfairness. They just give in to the pressure of society to get married," Pal remarked.

I said, "You made a brave decision by standing up to him. Dowry isn't just a one-time thing; they keep demanding more even after marriage. If we give in once, they'll keep asking. On the other hand, if we don't meet their demands, it can lead to domestic violence. It's important to keep your money safe from such people and families in society. Even if you can afford it, it's still a NO. I want to decide what I get in my marriage, not have others tell me what I need."

"The ones who beg for dowry, give them alms, not your daughter," I declared.

Pal sighed, and shared, "I remember as a small child, my maternal grandma often told my mom, you have a girl, better start saving." I was very curious why she said that. Growing up, once when she made the same statement of saving up for me, I asked, "Nani, why do you always ask my mother to save for me? Being a girl child, why do you insist on this?

My Nani made me sit beside her and said, 'Look, my father gave so much in dowry for my marriage, moving forward your grandfather and I gave so much in dowry to your mom in marriage. It is customary in our society to give a dowry to the girl child in her marriage. One cannot accumulate so much wealth in a short time, and therefore I keep telling your mom to accumulate wealth for your dowry. This is a very tedious process and often parents break their back in gathering the dowry, only to give away their precious daughter as well as their life's savings. These are hard facts and have been customary since ages and cannot be challenged.'

I had heard all this for years, and the point that it breaks the parents back in accumulating wealth for their daughter's marriage did not fit into my values. I decided, I will never encourage dowry, even if it means I have to get married late, or not marry at all."

Pal's pitch raised as she declared, "I had decided I will search for someone who accepts me for what I am, without seeing what dowry I can afford. We are educated, smart, independent, and capable of taking care of ourselves. Why do these guys feel they are doing a favour by marrying us?

Neither mine nor your parents are someone who supports the dowry system at any point or to anyone. We have always been against it. Taking and giving dowry are both crimes. There are parents who have mercilessly killed their daughters for the fear of giving dowry. So many girls have lost their lives just because of these people who think they deserve the bride's money for their sons."

"You know Pal, a friend of mine hails from a community that gives 7-8 layers of diamond necklace to the girl in her wedding. Rather, it is the guy's demand that the girl's parents give the best to the girl, as it is after all for her.

What if a bride doesn't want diamonds? What if her parents can't afford diamonds? Will the guy still marry?

Cars, motorbikes, gold, diamonds, cash, and the list is ever upgrading." I shared.

"If a guy has a straight spine and is well settled and self-sufficient, he will not depend on his bride's riches. We have families that raise sons educating them that asking for dowry is their birthright as they are boys. What if the bride decides to keep all her post-marriage earnings to herself, or her parents and not her husband and in-laws? All we need is a change in mindset. We need a new way of upbringing. We need to learn to be self-reliant," Pal stated.

"I have heard, you don't know what you have until you have lost it, and so I am glad you lost him. This proposal came as an interest of love, yet, the dominant message was, 'LOVE for SALE.' This proposal came with a price tag which was in no way acceptable." I exclaimed.

Chapter 15
The Good-Looking Guy

Pari, "I was introduced to this guy on a matrimonial app. He was an architect and had own architectural practice, and it was a growing organization. He was one of the people I met who wanted to make his mark in business, all by his own virtue. He was not dependent on his family to supply him or support him for his work and life, and this description about him in his profile inspired me to meet him.

Soon we decided to meet. Although he looked very average in the photograph, he had a captivating personality that exuded both charm and confidence. He came across as a very down-to-earth person. He was amiable to talk to and did not have any high demands or expectations of a life partner. He liked reading newspapers and I found this very intriguing. 'People in our generation read anything else but newspapers,' I told him, 'I do not have the patience to read all the news or scroll through the infinite pages in a newspaper and hence I don't read it.'

'You don't have to read the entire newspaper, only what pertains to your profession, or what affects you as a citizen of your country,' he suggested.

'Alright, current affairs and me are either side of the coin. Please give up on convincing me,' I replied, and we smiled.

I observed as his full shirt sleeve shifted, he had a tattoo on his left hand, near the wrist joint. Curiously, I asked him, 'What is your tattoo about?' He pulled up his sleeve and showed me. It read - Estd. 1987. He shared, 'That's my birth year, and the tattoo means Established in 1987.'

'Do you have any more tattoos?' I asked curiously.

'Yes, I have another on my back. Do you want me to show it to you?' Pal replied flushed. 'No, no thank you. That's fine.'

In fact, I wanted to see the tattoo, however with me asking to see the tattoo, the guy should not have any wrong intentions. Pari, I immediately thought about our conversation about telling guys to remove their shirts in the first meeting. This one, self-volunteered.

He insisted, 'Wait, let me show you.' While I thought he was really removing his shirt, he opened his phone picture gallery and showed me a photo of a tattoo. It was a huge tattoo of Shiva with his third eye open.

Pal messaged me- "Pari, I asked him to share the tattoo picture with me. I want to show it to you for your confirmation. The Shiva's tattoo started on the back and covered his forearm.

By the way, I have bombarded you with messages and there is more. Our conversations are going well, and we find each other suitable marriage types. Although in the back of my mind, I continuously thought about the tattoo.

Pari, I missed a beat thinking was this your vision of the Shiva Tattoo?

Now, he wants to introduce me to his cousins saying they are eager to see me. He asked if we could have a video call with them. Although it was too early, I agreed.

When he introduced me to his cousins over the phone, almost everyone said that I have the best catch from their family. They all held him in high regard and praised his good looks.

I was not sure how to react. I was never after a person's wealth or looks. I wanted a person with whom I could relate. Someone who would understand me, care for me, and respect the person I am. I just smiled and replied to his cousins, 'So he is.'

Today he broached the topic, 'You think we should speak to our parents now? I am ready to meet your parents.'

I was overwhelmed hearing this, and I admitted, 'So am I.'

With a heart full of optimism, he introduced me to his family by showing my photographs and horoscope. I too did the same. We were envisioning a seamless blend of our families too.

Our families met, and the discussion was so positive that they even discussed a tentative date for our engagement. His mother was not part of this meeting. I remember him talking to me a lot of times about how his mother and elder sister were dear to him. The fact that they were not here on such an important and deciding day of their son's life made me wonder.

When my parents asked him why his mother did not come to the meeting. His face flushed and he replied, 'She is keeping unwell.'

Our horoscopes matched 36 on 36 points, and we are declared an extraordinary couple by the astrologer. I had already read the charts, however now the tattoo haunts me because his Mom and sister were not involved in the meeting.

I was scrolling his chats and came across the photo of his tattoo which he had sent long ago, and she had missed seeing it before.

Is it the right tattoo? I am sending it to you. Is this the tattoo you had a vision of?" Pal concluded.

I was busy with my lectures and could not check my phone the entire day. I reverted a few hours after the lecture.

While Pal waited for my revert, she could sense something amiss, as by now. Pal tried to reach the guy. He was not responding to her calls. First, she thought he must be busy, however after two days of no communication Pal started contemplating. The tentative engagement date was fixed and was to be finalized depending on the availability of the venue. But why was he not responding?

I reverted the same day seeing Pal's message.

"The guy is not accessible to calls. Though I am puzzled, I chose to focus on the joyous occasion ahead. A sense of foreboding is creeping into my heart. I am scared. My parents have started asking questions as the engagement preparations are on." Pal said apprehensively.

"Pal, hold your breath for what I am going to say. Although the guy has the Shiva tattoo, this Shiva tattoo is different from what I saw. This one is with the third eye, and the one I saw is with a Trishul. The place of the tattoo also does not match. I am sure and can safely conclude this is not the man in my vision."

My words were enough to give Pal courage and face the fact that since he is not the right guy, this thing is going to end.

Pal decided to go see him in his office the next day since he was not responding to her calls. She messaged me about this and said she will update me soon.

Pal called to let me know what happened.

"I landed in his office. He was tied up with a client. I waited for an hour for him to be free. When he saw me, his face flushed. He called me to his cabin, and I expected to hear the worst so far.

He directly came to the point, 'It's my mother and sister. They are not ready for this marriage. They think I am so good looking; I can get a better girl as my life partner. They think your complexion is too wheatish to suit my fair complexion and that we won't look like a good match together.'

I sank into my chair, taking the gravity of the situation. I had creases on my forehead and was fuming with what I just heard, 'Wow, people still sit with shade cards to check marriage compatibility.' I couldn't help telling him that.

We were quiet for a while and he muttered, 'I didn't know how to convey this to you and hence I avoided you. I made attempts to bridge the gap between my mother's expectations and my desire for a future with you. I am facing a dilemma of choosing between familial expectations and personal fulfilment, a difficult decision I am unable to make. I think our family always thinks good for us. I hope you understand me.'

Although I was aware he is not the one as per Pari's vision, his comments on my wheatish colour hurt me. After all, beneath the skin I am an individual as any fair skinned one is.

I replied, 'For me these words sound hollow. You have been with me all through and liked me for who I am. I am sad for the commitment you have broken today on the virtue of your good looks. You make me feel otherwise. Although, I am not here to hear you or your mother's opinion of what you think of me. I was here for an answer, and I got mine.

Beautiful, I don't know if I am by any standards, but I am certainly courageous. I am responsible. I am committed to my word. If you had answered my call and given me your opinion back then, me and my parents would not have made efforts to finalize the engagement. Stand for yourself! It's high time. After all, you are thinking about marriage and not inviting people for your birthday.'

I left his office without even saying goodbye.

Pari, why are we still stuck on fairness and good looks when eventually it's the good heart that matters?" Pal asked, sounding a bit sad.

"Because people are shallow, and they want shallow things. It's always the outer beauty that matters to them. Like they want to flaunt their partner for the world. Beauty will fade one day. If you are happy and beautiful inside, you automatically shine outside." I replied.

"I am sick of looking for my dream man. For all his charm and charisma, this guy lacked the autonomy to make decisions about his own life. The prospect of marrying into a situation where external opinions held more importance than our dreams and promises." Pal proclaimed angrily.

"Pal, some people are like clouds when they disappear, it's a beautiful day. Just breathe. You are a free bird," I told her.

"A successful and fulfilling marriage required both partners to have a say in their lives, to shape their journey together based on their shared values and aspirations. I cannot fathom a future where our decisions are constantly under the scrutiny of external influences, particularly if those influences were more concerned with appearances than genuine happiness." Pal said apprehensively.

"You are right Pal, no one is spared of this, you see. There was an instance where an aunty came to see me from Kashmir. Apparently, she was seeking a bride for her son. She was from a business family in Kashmir, and they had rose farms for generations. They were financially well off like my parents and she came to know about me from a relative and decided to come see me.

The lady had a flawless milky white complexion, and her skin was so radiant and beautiful that she seemed to use some make-up.

She knew about my divorce status and was open-minded enough and accepting. She told me about her son and his late-night parties and that bringing him a bride might curtail all of that. She asked me questions and seemed to be very warm and easy to converse with.

So, you need someone who can tame your wild son, I thought and yet asked her, 'Aunty what make-up have you applied, you look radiant?'

She laughed when I asked her this and replied, 'This is my original, natural skin, and in Kashmir, we all have such radiant skin. We are all fair, and fairness comes in shades of milky white, peachy, pale, blush, and it's God's gift to us. The girls back in Kashmir are very beautiful and have all the good looks.'

I wondered about them for a while and thought why aunty would come all the way to Mumbai to search for a bride for her son when she can get him married to a beautiful and educated girl locally.

As she planned to leave, she told me, 'I bless you with all the happiness, and may you stay happy always.'

This was an obvious indication for me that she is not considering me for her son, which I was happy about. All that I could think was, it must be my wheatish skin colour.

We are all drawn to good looks and fairness, and then we cannot deny the mentality of the people who still feel fairness creams are a boon for girls to look good and secure a good husband.

Even when the government has banned the use of 'Fairness' word on products, the mentality of people wouldn't change."

Pal agreed to it and calmed down.

Chapter 16
The International Guy

Pal called me as soon as she got back home from her official trip. I too was traveling at that time. Pal was vulnerable to the happenings in her life and blurted out.

"Pari, Why am I drawn to unexpected things?" She questioned me angrily over the phone.

"What did you do now, Pal?" I inquired and she told me all that happened.

"I have known this guy since ages now, he was a friend's friend and is a very sorted and accomplished guy. Coming from a third-tier city, he had made a mark for himself by securing a job in a top IT Company. He was deputed in their London office.

It all started when I wanted to gather some knowledge about his IT skill sets for recommending to a cousin and called him. I did know that this seemingly mundane act would unravel much beyond friendship. He helped me with all the necessary information I needed. After that on some pretext, we stayed in touch with each other. In some time, it became a daily matter where we had to chat at least once a day. We had become used to each other. He took our virtual friendship around the wonders of London. He painted pictures of picturesque landscapes, ancient architecture, and the famous walks of London. I found myself enchanted by the tales of this distant land, especially captivated by the narrator who made them more interesting.

We pledged to meet in person when he was in India. The promise created a sense of anticipation and excitement for the day when he would return to India, and we could finally meet.

His family lived on the outskirts of the town and as decided I went to meet him. I also arranged a client meeting around that place.

After my official meeting concluded successfully, I went to his place as he had invited me for lunch with his family, an offer I gladly accepted. This morning when I arrived at his house, I was greeted by the welcoming smiles of his family.

We all sat down on the mats on the kitchen floor to have our meal. The food was served on banana leaves. The aroma of home-cooked delicacies wafted through the air. However, the atmosphere took an unexpected turn when, in the midst of the meal, he made a bold declaration to everyone.

'I want to marry her,' he announced, looking at me. I choked on his statement as it caught me off guard. I suddenly felt tightness in my chest. His expression was overwhelming with happiness, as he had grown to love me over the course of our interactions. However, his mother remained composed, showing little inclination towards or against the idea. As his words echoed in my ears, I felt a mix of emotions—surprise, uncertainty, and a hint of embarrassment. What struck me the most was that he hadn't sought my opinion on the matter. The decision to share such a significant aspiration seemed to be made alone, leaving me in a state of mild shock. I wasn't sure how to react. I decided to ignore it at this point, finish our meal, and then talk to him in person.

Despite the suddenness of the situation, I couldn't deny that I was fond of him as a good friend. Over the past few months, our connection had grown deeper, and his affectionate gestures had left an imprint on my heart. Seeing that he cared for me so deeply tugged at the strings of my emotions. Although I never asked him for the tattoo as I never thought about marrying him.

After the meal, eager to continue the surprises, he led me to his room. With an infectious enthusiasm, he began presenting me with an array of carefully chosen gifts—tokens of his affection and, perhaps, symbols of a future he envisioned.

'Take this, and this, and even this,' he exclaimed, his eyes gleaming with happiness.

Before I could fully process the moment, he, with a boyish grin, excused himself and left the room. Sooner, sensing the need for a formal gesture, he gathered his entire family around me. His mother, a figure of authority, approached me. In her hands, she held a loaded envelope, its contents were a mystery. As she extended the envelope toward me, he said, 'Accept it.' Confused and intrigued, I hesitated for a moment. The weight of the envelope seemed to carry the responsibility of tradition and customs, unfamiliar to me. He was, however, persistent, and repeated, 'It is Shagan for your marriage to me.'

I told him, 'I want to speak to you in person.'

He jokingly uttered with a wink, 'Yes, we will talk in person too.'

I found myself at a crossroads. The notion of shagan, a symbolic gesture for a union that I had not fully comprehended, left me feeling both honoured and uncertain. His family, sensing my hesitation, offered reassurance. 'Ok. Accept it as a gift from us,' they suggested, 'as you have come for the first time to our house.'

The room erupted in smiles and a sense of joy as I took the envelope.

I insisted to him for a personal dialogue, but he asked, 'About our honeymoon destination?'

'A good sense of humour makes a man handsome. You are already handsome, but what's happened to your sense of humour?' I declared.

'What happened? Why are you cross with me? We had such a good time together sometime back,' he asked.

'How can you announce marriage without even asking me?' I inquired.

'Oh that! Let's discuss it. I am flying back from your city. Come join me in my cab. We will talk on the way to the airport. It was a wonderful day so far and my sense and humour both are tired now.'

In hindsight I thought he was after all a highly educated and settled guy and my parents wouldn't object to a fine guy like him. Yet, how could he announce something without my permission?

His mother's face went sour looking at me. She was going to drop him at the airport. Seeing me coming along, she didn't seem so happy.

On the other hand, I thought, was I aware that she would be alone, I would not have tagged along. Finally, after the farewell, we settled into the cab, and he took his place beside the driver, and I sat behind him next to his mother.

His mother, a woman of calculation, broke the silence with an unexpected question. 'You travelled here for your work, you mentioned. Now, these travel expenses, will you bill the company?' She inquired; her eyes were keenly observant. Naively, I responded with a simple 'yes,' my mind still lingering on the events of the day.

As the words left my lips, her intention dawned upon me. His mother was not merely making casual conversation. She was subtly probing into the details of my travel, hinting at something more beneath the surface. In my innocence, I had inadvertently suggested that I would be billing the company for my travel expenses when I was traveling free with them in their cab.

The guy did not say anything to his mom who was asking such leading questions.

He momentarily asked the cab driver to halt as he wanted to withdraw money from an ATM, his mother seized the moment, and turned to me, her eyes sharp with scrutiny. 'How much do you earn?' She inquired, her question cutting through the air like a blade.

I hesitated for a moment. The question was not merely about my income; it was about an evaluation of my worth.

Gathering my composure, I replied, 'I make 85K a month.'

She gave an unsatisfactory look and asked, 'Where do you stay?'

I answered, 'Mumbai suburbs,' and her face was not appealing to my answer, and she derogatorily remarked, 'Oh there, the crowded Mumbai suburbs with matchbox houses. My Son owns a big apartment in London. He has bought it outright.'

Her response, delivered with a calculated tone, was a revelation in itself. To that she added, 'My son has a very different lifestyle than yours. He earns in lakhs per month. He would get many girls in our community who understand his real value. He is my diamond. I have many proposals in line for him. There are some of the best girls in our community looking to marry him. He is a steal for them.' She opened her purse and showed me some pics on her phone.

While proudly scrolling them she said, 'See, I have all the girl's photos lined up for him. I was going to show him the photos. I am quiet because you are here. Although, he will never go out of my word,' she asserted.

He has achieved so much very early in life. Her words carried a protective undertone, a motherly defence of her son's worth in the face of an unfamiliar outsider.

As she continued, I felt I was not just a passenger in the cab; I was an unexpected intruder into the carefully crafted plans for his future. She continued, 'He is very naïve and excited at times about things, and I would make him understand. I thought it was only the two of us who were traveling back, and you came in unannounced.'

The tension in the cab grew palpable as her words lingered, a subtle warning. 'Don't dream about whatever he told you this afternoon. Don't even consider the shagun I gave you with my own hands. It does not mean anything,' she concluded, her tone unyielding.

His mother had laid bare her intentions, leaving me to grapple with cultural differences, familial expectations, and that my presence was an unexpected twist in their carefully scripted life.

In her calculating gaze, 'value' wasn't just about his personal qualities; it was a veiled reference to the dowry he could potentially attract as a well-educated and settled boy.

He returned just then, looked at me and asked, 'Are you alright? Why do you look so pale?'

I replied, 'I am just fine.'

'Pal, can you lend me some cash for the airport? I am unable to withdraw money somehow to pay for the cab. I have foreign currency otherwise. I will return your money when I reach London.' He requested.

I opened my purse and gave him the cash, and told him to keep it, you don't need to return it back. Additionally, I also took out the shagun envelope and looking at his Mom, placed it in his hand.

I could not control it and revealed in a firm tone looking at his Mom, 'He asked me to come along. I did not impose on him.' I corrected her. 'I HAD NO CLUE your son WOULD ASK ME FOR MARRIAGE, and I am myself wondering why. I am here because I wanted to discuss with him why he announced something without asking my consent and by making a scene. I am not here to interfere between you mother and son.'

I looked at him and stated, 'Your Mom has a lot of girls who would want to marry you. Goodluck!!'

Saying I took my bag and moved out of the cab. He came after me. I told him, this is not the time, you will miss your flight. So, he went back to his cab and went away.

I hailed another cab back home and blocked him out from every social media and contacts.

I want his mother to know I am just not any girl who was behind her son for money. Whatever money I made; I was proud of myself for earning it.

He was a genuine man with a heart that beats for love and was now a chapter of my past. My only intention was to meet him, and here I was.

His mother, who is a better judge of his life and deserves his company, would now have him back. For me, letting go was the ultimate expression of our friendship. His mother had no respect for me, she misunderstood the person I was. Rather she did not even try to understand me, and this would be an ongoing and nagging challenge if I ever got married to him. Some indications are very clear, even if the proposal seems right.

How can a person who makes decisions without my consent even consider what I am saying? He will forget me too soon when his mother gets him proposals she likes. As it is, we were never romantically involved for any of us would have heartbreak.

I am just questioning the marriage system and the family approach in such situations. It sucks. It makes you feel like a criminal. Like whatever you have made of your life, your studies, your job, your status, your salary, your self-respect all is questioned by people who are not even worth evaluating you, or even have achieved what you have. Because you are someone about to get married, you are interrogated, evaluated, and sometimes even insulted.

It's not worth the deal. After all, my self-respect is above everything, and the day I compromise it, I will not be myself." Pal admitted.

"Also, I am done dealing with the guys' families. You were right Pari, we should concentrate only on the guy, and not his family. Here everyone has a different expectation of you. So, even if the guy likes you, you do not have an assured entry into the family, unless they all evaluate you and approve of you. More often the family played the villain. I wonder about the guys who marry against their family wishes. They must face the brunt of their family, while trying to secure their love life and marriage." Pal mentioned.

"They can go to any length to make you feel unwelcome and unwanted. I have lived it all in my marriage. I do not hold opinions merely on my fantasies. These are lived truths. I have worked hard to get this key to success and people thought I was just picking up locks." I concluded.

Chapter 17
The Tattoo Guy

On a warm summer morning, my dad's phone rang. The call was from a lady who stated, "I got your reference from the Bund Centre. I know your daughter is of a marriageable age and I am calling on behalf of my brother for whom we are seeking a bride."

My Dad replied – "Yes. I am looking to get my daughter married."

She replied, "Apparently, your daughter and my brother are colleagues. Although your daughter is unaware about this proposal. My brother and Pal work together and he is interested in her profile and hence I am calling you. I will send you his profile. Pal knows him as a mere colleague. You both could check his details."

Dad got all the details of Vinayak along with his pictures from his sister. First, I was surprised and I told dad, "Tell them NO already. I need a break from these marriage proposals."

Mom composed me and explained, "Pal, marriage is not child's play. You need to be calm and wait for the right partner. After all, they say, marriages are made in heaven, and your angel is yet to enter your life. Wait for him!"

My dad now declared as my mom listened quietly, "Nobody will say anything to her - if she is not interested in meeting the guy - she will not make the correct decision. Let her heart decide what she wants. We will never force her, especially if she is not interested.

I will inform them - you can check other proposals. My daughter is not ready for marriage at this time."

Pal called me the very next moment and shared, "Honestly, I am surprised with this proposal as it is from my office. Currently I am not looking for any proposals. There is a volcano inside me. I am facing the heat of both my professional & personal life. Professionally I am feeling very disturbed with the office politics, which is sucking my energy. Personally, there is no respite. I am disturbed as nothing is falling in place as expected. I had convinced my mind that marriage was not my cup of tea. I even told my mom. I think I am not meant for marriage.

By the way, I called up to talk about my colleague Vinayak. He has sent a marriage proposal. I don't know who he is and it's freaking me." Pal shared.

"Wow!! So, who is this new character in your life? Having met so many prospects for marriage I don't remember names." I asked.

I said to Pari, knowing she is the one who will listen and understand, "I have crossed the age of 31, and today's men want women who are below 30 yrs. of age for marriage. Our society is such that they have made rules about the age of marriage, and again the many expectations of the guys and their families. I am pissed about meeting guys now. I don't want to go out and meet another guy, understand him, and end up breaking my heart time and again. Either I am not fulfilling their expectations, or they just want someone out of this world. None of these guys asked what I wanted?"

The following weekend ....

Pal called me to update.

She shared, "I went to the Bund centre. It is a cultural committee for our caste that organizes events. I was surprised to see Vinayak there.

He confronted me and apologized saying, 'I was not aware you are not looking to get married now. You must think how I got your details. You are a part of the Bund Community, and so is my sister. My sister got your details from there. She showed me your profile along with others as suitable matches for me. This was a couple of months back. Then I saw you at my office and figured out we work together. I have observed you over the months now. After which I asked my sister to contact your parents. Please don't think I am stalking you or will pursue you further without your will. My intentions are clear, I want to marry you because I like you. It's not a random decision. I do not want you to hasten either. Take your time. Rest assured, no one will ever learn in the office about this proposal. Relax.' Saying he moved behind and left.

I kept silent because a part of me somewhere trusted him, while on the other hand, I have this part that is lost and least interested in marriage or seeing men. I was fighting my inner demons and was not ready to accept someone."

Days passed and over time, Pal was observing Vinayak, although she had rejected him. She had never met a guy before who was sensitive, and at the same time practical. He knew what he wanted, and did not make Pal uncomfortable about it.

Pal was wary because of the experiences she had in the past. She did not want to feel good about a proposal and see it not working eventually.

It is better to be straight and withdrawn when one is unsure. At least she was not giving someone hope or hurting herself.

Vinayak and she crossed paths in the office, and he politely wished her and went ahead. He was not the person who would try to make an impression on her or dissuade her. The fact that everything was normal back in the office, no curious glances, no gossip made her comfortable that Vinayak had kept it all to himself.

His good behaviour made her think about him. Somewhere this attention deficiency was playing on Pal's mind. She wished Vinayak would speak to her some more other than work related stuff, and she would get to know him better.

"He doesn't make any advances to talk. He just exchanges pleasantries and goes away," Pal told me, a hint of frustration in her voice. We have been greeting each other and sometimes ignoring each other too. Apparently, I feel a connection with him. It's strange, we don't even know each other well," she exclaimed, her voice filled with confusion.

"If it's making so much of a difference to you, just ask him out," I suggested, seeing her sudden interest, "Go meet him somewhere if you are so curious. Go for a coffee, spend some time together, just as colleagues, as acquaintances." I suggested.

"You remember the guy from my vision of your life partner? Vinayak seems to be like him, as you described tall, well-built. Although I haven't seen him myself, I can relate through whatever you say about him over the past one month. At least figure out if he has a tattoo or not. It will be easier to strike him off if he doesn't have one." I offered.

"Yes, you are right!" Pal admitted, her shoulders sagging as she realized I was not wrong.

Pal hesitated. Although we were on the phone, I could clearly visualize her shaking her head, while having a frown, biting the back of her pen sitting in her office cabin. She then shook her head and declared, "He doesn't have a tattoo."

I chuckled, trying to lighten the mood, and asked, "First stop chewing your pen and tell me, did you ever see him without a shirt to conclude he doesn't have a tattoo on his arm?"

"Who ever thought that a tattoo would become a reason to marry someone," Pal replied sarcastically, and we both burst into laughter, the tension easing between us.

As our laughter subsided, I mentioned, "Sometimes, connections are beyond physical attributes. Maybe it's something deeper, something we can't see but feel. Just meet him once and prove me wrong."

I felt Pal nodding her head slowly, with a thoughtful look on her face. The mystery of Vinayak lingered, and the bond she felt was undeniable, an enigma that was slowly beginning to unfold.

Some days later....

I was attending a class, my phone continuously beeped and vibrated. I could see it was my monster at crime trying to reach me. Figuring out her urgency, I went under the table and answered her call.

"You know what just happened today?" Pal blurted excitedly.

Pal seemed to be strong & composed, yet there was something remarkably different in her voice. I guessed it was hope. Her excitement had increased mine too. It was a feeling of finally getting the answer for a word problem which was long pending.

I whispered, "What happened?"

She replied, "It was a cheerful day, and you won't believe what just happened."

"Pal, you need to stop raising my adrenaline and start talking to me before I need a Doctor," I exclaimed.

Pal initiated, "I went to the office gym today, and finally decided to give some attention to myself." Pal's voice tinged with some big news, "I went early for my workout, and I noticed that Vinayak fellow was there too, wearing his gym clothes - a vest and track pants. He was far away and didn't see me coming in. As he was busy with his workout, I just took a glance and started with my treadmill. There are these huge mirrors on the wall where I can see people working out behind my back. I glanced at Vinayak in the mirror. Not that I wanted to.

I saw something remarkable—he had a tattoo on his shoulder arm. Guess what, the tattoo is of Shiva holding an intricately designed trishul. Just like the one you had a vision of. I was numb and stopped the treadmill I was standing on. My heart beat increased. I wanted to click the picture of his tattoo, but it would be inappropriate. Anyone seeing me taking pictures would feel I am stalking guys, and hence I refrained."

I felt a rush of excitement surge through me. "Pal, I told you, see," I declared, as I accidentally banged my head against the table. "Ouccchh," my scream echoed through the class, and my classmates knew it was Pari, the noisy one everywhere, and it was all normal after that.

Ignoring the bump and pain in my head, I continued to be under the table and talked to Pal as I couldn't wait for my session to get over. I continued to whisper, "You continue... I am listening," my voice full of anticipation.

"Pari, I could never see the tattoo before in his corporate attire," Pal continued, and I could fathom her eyes were wide with wonder. "It's hidden beneath his formal shirts. However, this time it was clear."

I leaned closer, eager to hear more. "So, is he just like the guy from my vision?" I asked, needing to reconfirm the details of the man. I sensed Pal nodding her head vigorously as she confirmed, "Yes, exactly as you described. Tall, well-built, gymming and health freak, toned muscles and now that Shiva tattoo—it's uncanny," Pal said.

A shiver ran down my spine. I sat down completely on the floor now, folding my legs, not interested in the class anymore. I had goosebumps as I exclaimed, "Oh wow, that's amazing." The pieces of the puzzle were falling into place. This was no coincidence. My vision was coming to life right before my eyes. I was happy for Pal and proud of myself.

"Isn't it enough that he has himself come with the proposal?" I asked.

"I was not expecting the universe to surprise me this way when I had given up on marriage." Pal sighed.

"What are you waiting for then? I think you should go talk to him and reconsider his proposal. Do not mention to him about the tattoo yet. Hold onto your horses and ask him out for coffee. Definitely this time it is not going to be a waste of time, effort, or energy. He is the soulmate you are seeking and let's see how it all unfolds," I suggested.

Very soon Pal resumed the conversation on marriage with Vinayak. They decided to meet over coffee and see how things go further.

When Pal returned from the first meeting, she called me instantly.

"How was the meeting?" I inquired.

"Very preliminary. We exchanged some information about each other about our likes, dislikes, hobbies, how he came to join my company and all. I want to meet him again. You know these first meetings are so superficial and goody-goody types." Pal mentioned.

"I bet he too is dying to meet you again," I proclaimed.

"Yes, you know he told me before too, take your time." Pal affirmed.

"Ya ya, he was implying, take your time to think about him. Poor fellow he must have lost so many kilos running on your mind all these days. I am sure you might be doing all the naughty stuff in your head," I implied pulling her leg.

"Haha, who is naughty here? And you know I cannot kill you as you are one good devil that came to my life," Pal confessed.

"Vinayak and I continued to behave the same way in the office, exchanged greetings with a smile, and spoke about work. Nobody was aware of the spark that had triggered between us. We continued meeting over coffee." Pal mentioned.

On one weekend,

"Vinayak told me about his personal life and some things that I did not expect from him," Pal sounded mushy.

"Like what? Tell me fast as I ate patience in my breakfast," I exclaimed.

"He told me about his home. How he bought a home without informing his parents and by arranging the funds on his own," Pal shared.

"OK, looks like he is hardworking and makes his own decisions. I like that. I am not sure whose boxes he is ticking, yours or mine. He seems promising." I chuckled.

Pal laughed her lungs out. It was one more tick in her so-called mental list of her perfect guy.

Pal narrated, "I asked him, what was your intention to buy this house, just an investment in the property or any other reason? Have you bought the home because you were intending to get married? You know right, the girls these days usually want their partner to have their own home before marriage."

He shared, 'I was not prepared to buy a new house and was on the go with rental homes. Rather, I was tired of the constant shifting. I intend to get married and settle down and have my family. At least my partner should have her space. He was straight in disclosing his financials, and also showed me his salary slip. Although, he did not ask me for mine.'

I replied, 'I like your honesty. You are an open book to me. I am not sure what the next chapter is going to be in your book, but I am sure the chapter won't be incomplete.'

He looked in my eyes and smiled, 'I want to be clear about everything, and I think this information could help you make a better decision, whatever it is. Again, there is no hurry,' he said, assuring me.

I mentioned to him that I still need some time, and he obliged.

He then told me that he is fond of eating and cooks on and off."

"Pal, at least the questions now changed to statements from, Can you cook to I can cook. I am happy to know." I said.

"No. In fact I told him, I can cook only lentils and rice, and he commented, 'Cooking is not his criteria for shortlisting someone. There are options we can have if one can't cook. We can have a cook or cook together.'"

"Really? He said that!! He deserves an award for this from me," I declared, overjoyed at this too good to be true situation.

"Pal, I hope he is not just wooing both of us." I expressed my doubts.

"By the way, he wore a t-shirt today and the Shiva tattoo was peeping from beyond his sleeves. I asked him to sound oblivious, do you have a tattoo, and he showed me a picture of his whole tattoo. I told him, Nice tattoo and he shared that he is a devotee of Lord Shiva, and thus the tattoo. I had mentally reconfirmed about the tattoo now." Pal mentioned.

"Vinayak also mentioned that his parents are orthodox, and I will have to consider that.

Although you do not need to change for them. This gave me a bit of peace knowing there aren't many expectations of me to change. However, there was something else dwelling in my mind. I want to see the house where I would stay if I consented to marry Vinayak.

When I mentioned to Vinayak about my desire, he was momentarily silent and then mentioned, 'A girl does not go to her husband's house before marriage, according to our culture and customs. My parents might object to your coming home. However, you leave it to me, let me see how I can snoop you in.'

Pari, he is making efforts. He seems to be a man who makes his own decisions and finds solutions, he will definitely work on this too?" Pal mentioned.

Pal called me a week later and said, "It is Ganpati festival time, and Vinayak has invited my parents and me stating, 'We have Ganpati festival at home and you come along with your parents to seek blessings. This way you can also see the house. I will handle everything here.'

He respects my wishes." Pal stated.

"Pal, see he did it." I confirmed.

A few days later...

"Pari, He has a lovely home. More than that, I'm happy that he kept my wish of seeing the house before marriage. I knew there must be objections as he mentioned. Yet, he ensured it happened as I wanted. It all looks dreamy."

I was super excited to know how things were progressing and expressed, "It's all true Pal, your wish is finally coming true."

Finally, Pal and Vinayak met a couple of times, and I could see she had developed a liking for him now. Having had such experiences in the past, she did not want to jump into marriage. She wanted to be very sure.

Pal had her checks and gave her consent for marriage. When both the family members came together to fix the marriage, Pal's father asked the obvious question of dowry, which is so prevalent in their community.

Pal called me to update on the talks between Vinayak and her family. She said, "Vinayak boldly stated, 'My family and I do not encourage and want any dowry. I love your daughter and just want to marry her.'

Pari, my parents were surprised and could not believe it all and looked at me. I assured them that what Vinayak mentioned was his own decision. I blushed looking at Vinayak and acknowledged his gesture. After all, it seemed too good to be true to find someone who thinks differently from the rest. Especially when you have met people with varying mindsets for marriage."

Pal's engagement ceremony was something that was to be organized by the bride's party as the tradition goes, and they were solely responsible for bearing the expenses.

"Pari, I do not want to financially burden Dad with these expenses and thus I told Vinayak, what if we skip this ritual and do it on the wedding day, or do it at home just between our two families?

The functions are a waste of money. My happiness is to be with you. I will be wearing artificial jewellery for our marriage. You know the custom of wearing five or seven gold necklaces. I don't want to invest in gold, which I might not even wear in the future."

His instant reply was, 'Pal, I am marrying you and not your jewellery. You should be comfortable as much as you can, after all it is going to be our special day.'

Pari, my marriage is finally scheduled for February 2020, and I wouldn't have done it without you.

You had better book your tickets in advance. Afterall, you are my only bridesmaid."

While the marriage preparations were on, Pal called me and said vulnerably, "Pal, it's finally happening!!

Vinayak has announced between the two families, let us keep the ring ceremony just between our two families and we can have it here at home. No need to call people or book a hall. Throughout he never mentioned that it was Pal's wish. He implied it as his decision."

"Pari, do you know, on the engagement day, amidst the lovely gathering of families, Vinayak's sisters while chatting with me asked, 'When are you getting your nose pierced? You know how important it is as a tradition for the bride to wear a nose ring on the wedding day.'

I replied, 'I am not fond of nose piercings and nose rings.'

Vinayak was around and intervened, 'It's completely Pal's wish. Nothing will go against her will. We can have clip-on nose pins, he said looking at his sisters.'

Pal smiled and said, 'Yes, I did mention this to him.'

Hearing this, Vinayak's sisters acknowledged it quietly."

Chapter 18
Pre-Marriage

It's truly said, 'Marriages are made in heaven.'

I flew down from Australia for Pal's wedding.

While we were catching up on the wedding shopping, Pal said, "Oh my God Pari, I have only fallen in love with a guy who has all the qualities which I admired and aspired to in my life partner. A dream guy indeed!"

"My vision was for a reason. I just don't make stories from nowhere," I declared.

"When you know this, I hope you know your beach guy is also waiting for you. If he is the guy from our vision, that means he is out there in real life and waiting for you. Stop waiting for Adein, he is not coming back. Seek the one who is seeking you," Pal urged.

"Pal, we will talk about my beach guy later. You focus on your wedding for now." I suggested.

Just before the wedding day, Pal called me to her room and said, "Pari, I am getting cold feet."

"Don't tell me you are thinking of withdrawing from the marriage." I asked apprehensive.

"Oh No!! Not like that!" Pal replied.

"Then what?" I asked.

"Pari, my parents have done a lot for this day to happen successfully. They are doing all this for my happiness. They have booked a good venue, have the best decor and even food arranged for the people who will attend the wedding. Hope all goes well." Pal said overwhelmed.

"Pal, if you are worrying about the people who will come for your wedding, stop worrying right now. They will come, observe everything, eat, waste, comment, take selfies and be jealous. Then they would also criticize the bride's clothes, her hairstyle, and makeup, the arrangements made, the sweet and less variety in food, the gold you are wearing, and even the honeymoon destination you have chosen.

Oh, she is going to Munnar, not Maldives.

These are the people we call society, and they have only one goal- to criticize. Don't think much. You just be the happiest bride ever." I persuaded Pal.

Chapter 19
Haldi Ceremony

I accompanied Pal's family members to take haldi to the groom's house as a tradition. The entire house was decorated with flowers and smelled of incense sticks and camphor. His cousins and family members were all dressed in themed outfits. The women of the house were busy and were arranging stuff for the rituals.

Among the festivities and the happy faces, I was stunned to see a revelation. Vinayak sat on a low stool with a carpet on it. There was haldi in a container and lit lanterns kept in front of him as the women negotiated who would start the ritual.

He stood there in front of me, wearing a simple white vest and loose pyjamas, and something about him caught my attention immediately. His shoulder and one arm were exposed. On his hand, there was a tattoo of Lord Shiva, strikingly detailed and vibrant. The image of Shiva, with its intricate design.

What amazed me the most was the sheer similarity between this moment and a vision I had seen earlier. It was as though reality had perfectly mirrored the vision I had experienced before - down to the smallest details. The clarity of the tattoo, everything was just as I had seen it in my mind. It felt surreal and I was in awe seeing my vision turning to reality.

Once we were done with the ritual, I called Pal and told her what just unfolded in front of me. Pal was assured and said, "Our shortlisting criteria was the tattoo, and I am glad you could see it and confirm yourself. Wohoo, we did it Pari!!"

Chapter 20
The Wedding Day

Pal looked like an Indian goddess, in the golden saree, and matching imitation jewellery - beautiful and resplendent. She had all the attention on her that day. Vinayak looked at her in awe.

It all resonated with my vision of the south Indian wedding Pal would have. It was like my pieces of vision were falling in place one after the other.

Pal thought of all that she had been through in the process of searching for a guy and here she was finally getting married. She looked at Vinayak and expressed her gratitude for making this happen.

Three Months Later...

It was Covid time and despite wanting to meet and talk, we could not. I was back in Australia and Pal a newlywed. With lockdown, she had everyone around her through the day, and as a new bride, she had her set of responsibilities.

I messaged Pal, "It's hard to find a friend who is cute, sexy, loving, generous, caring, and smart. My advice is - Don't lose me."

She called me immediately.

"Looks like heaven is treating you well that you have forgotten this hell," I confronted her.

"I am still a hell person giving you company in hell. I am not leaving you, my monster. But you see marriage changes a lot of things for a girl. Especially the initial years she has to give to her family. You might know better, Pari." Pal exclaimed.

"Yes Pal, I was myself secluded from my family after marriage because I was understanding things at my ex-husband's house. I was busy cooking new things for him. I was learning about my in-laws' customs and traditions. I was basically trying to make my position in his family, to the extent that I was declared a housewife - good for nothing." I uttered.

"Aww my baby, why do you say that?" Pal said oozing her dose of love for me.

I continued, "I was not allowed to go out and work. Just staying at home, cooking, and taking responsibility for the house was the duty I had no other role to play. Because I took a break from my job just to give more time at home, to nurture my new family, and what did this lead to? I was considered good for nothing sitting at home, and after a certain time, I even refrained from seeking a job. Why do you need a job? Girls don't go out to work. Stay at home and look after the house, and my parents, he would say. I think it is not wrong. He had his identity, and I had mine. Unfortunately, I lost it after marrying him. Taking up responsibilities is a part of a process, but losing yourself in the process is like killing yourself. Although I had agreed to follow his league, I realized I couldn't continue to kill myself any further in that house."

"You were so fiercely independent and earned well. Didn't you want to go back to work?" Pal asked.

"I did want to, and yet my love for my ex-husband stopped me. I felt how I could go beyond his words. If he has asked me to refrain from working it is his love. I was naive not to understand that he is not loving me but clipping my wings, bringing me under control. Slowly it all percolated to who I was calling and why." I explained.

"Oh, I am happy you are divorced now," Pal stated.

"I am happy Pal that you want to continue meeting your friends even after marriage. I wish I could have continued too. I wish I had opened my mouth then and spoken for what I want rather than letting my husband make decisions for me." I mentioned.

"Pari, we all have some setbacks in life, and that is how we learn. By facing our fears. I have seen you face your fears and evolve so much that today you are more confident and powerful than yesterday. I have seen you facing your fear by talking to men and now you have evolved so much that you know how to communicate with them and treat them. At one point you hated to speak to them and now you mingle with so many people, cultures and exchange laughter and happiness. I am happy for you.

You must know, I think I am living the bride's dream of a beautiful marriage. Vinayak is an amazing person.

However, one thing is disturbing. My parents-in-law behave with me in a certain way when my husband is around and otherwise when he is at work. I sometimes don't understand how to handle this and even tell Vinayak. After all they are his parents, and he might be offended." Pal shared.

"Pal, that's true. No one would want to hear anything against their parents. Even we won't like it. Men hardly face their wife's parents, and we live with their parents full-time, so there are many chances for difference of opinions in the latter.

I could never talk to Adain about the certain things his mother and sisters were doing to me. In fact, his silence was a punishment to me." I admitted.

"Well, it's so important that the man listens and evaluates both sides of the story. While his parents are important to him, a girl is getting married to him only by trusting him and his promises made to her. She had put her life at stake by deciding to marry him. She is leaving everything she has built so far, and moving into a new home, new people, and a completely new life.

Can in-laws not judge her and help her settle her home? Why the discrimination of - we don't do this at our house. This is not allowed. This is not accepted, and this is restricted. Why aren't they acceptable to some new things that the new bride might bring in? Our society is rigid to change. They will change but slowly and gradually." Pal urged.

"Congratulations on your arranged marriage. I am happy you are living your ideal dream marriage, at least most of it.

Pal, it's important that a man takes a stand, for what is right and what is not agreeable. Marriage is about two people sharing life and responsibilities. A man should consider himself as human and not God or a judge and pass a verdict. The responsibilities should be shared, and decisions should be discussed and taken. One might change and become a different person after a few years. One should stand by their commitment in a relationship and deliver. There will be a lot of forks in life, and yet you need to decide what is right." I said.

"Pari, Vinayak is supportive of me, unfortunately, I don't know how to address the issue of the difference in behaviour of his parents. Thus, I thought of speaking to you first before speaking to him." Pal mentioned.

"Wait for the right time, you will automatically get all our answers." I assured.

After some years.......

Pal has been happily married for a few years now.

One might think all the goody-goody romantic phase is over and now reality has set in.

Reality did set in...

Pal and Vinayak - The couple are taking care of each other and sharing responsibilities. Vinayak though a self-decision maker, now discusses with Pal before taking any big and small decision. He cooks food for her by referring to cooking video guides when she is running late from her office. For instance, he cooks biryani sealed with love and they eat it with their midnight talks, and laughter. He has kept the promise he made to Pal during their wedding, that I will stand with you and for you in thick and thin.

One day Pal admitted to me, "Your glimpses worked, Pari. You have shown me the way to the tattoo guy - my soulmate. I cannot thank the universe for helping me believe in true love.

I wait for amazing things to happen in your life now."

"Pari, I am living the life I had manifested. Now it's your turn. Can we start accepting applications for your partner in crime now?" Pal asked.

"The first orgasm my ex ever gave me was when he signed our divorce papers. I never dreamt that one day I will be a sexy divorcee, and today I am killing it. Bring it on!!" I confirmed.

Chapter 21
Our Voice

To All of Us

From vision to reasons Pal found her guy, even when it seemed late according to the society's standards. We did not bother. Although she gave up, in the end she was blessed with the right person at the right time and that's what I call the 'Divine Time.'

We all have hopes and aspirations about marriage and partners, and even if we are told 100 things about marriage, our experience is our very own and teaches us and guides us. So, do not be dejected, do not fall for society's age-old tradition and customs.

People will come and tell you their stories, honestly, it is all one trap, you should not be ensnared in it. This is their experience and their learning. This does not apply to us anyhow. Families under societal pressure make their children marry and then repent.

The reason for marriage failures might be different - The guy is not independent, the girl is asked to leave her career and settle at home, the family background is disturbed, the family is asking for dowry, the family members are not well educated and acceptable, and adjusting, and there are numerous reasons.

It is not about a love marriage or arranged marriage. It's about how you are wisely handling together the situations and challenges arising in a marriage. Marriage is all about ignoring the unwanted and accepting the right. The more flexible you are, the longer the relationship fosters. Following your heart and commitment is more important than blindly following some customs.

For society, you need to ease out, let people breathe and let them decide when to get married, rather than imposing on them a timeline.

As parents we can ensure that like our kids these are other's kids, and if your child is doing very well in life, don't be boastful about the entire thing as you don't know what scenario the other person comes from.

People are bothered about other people's marriages and often pry making unwanted statements and questions like - Oh you are not married yet; you are 30. You are not getting proposals? You won't get proposals after 25. It will be too late to have babies. Why don't you marry anyone?

Once they find the couple is married, there are a series of questions around having a baby. Some couples decide not to have kids, while some are unable to conceive due to medical reasons. Don't tag them as childless. It is entirely their outlook and decision to have a child. We need to stop asking them questions like, "Have you thought of a baby? When are you having a baby? One baby is not enough, you need to bring them some company. A mother is incomplete without a child, so on and so forth.

Nevertheless, society has nothing to do with you, your marriage, and your babies. They won't send you proposals, they are not a part of your baby making act, they are not the ones who are nursing and caring for your baby, they are not bearing your marriage expenses or even delivery expenses. Don't be their prey. Don't let them dictate how you should live your life. You should decide what you want and how you want to live your life.

With such incessant and unnecessary questions, there is surely a phase where one revolts, in return society says, you are rude, you don't know to respect people, you back answer. After all, we were trying to wish well for you.

Nobody asked them (society) to think good and interfere. Some marital relations are beautiful as they are, and they don't need the pepper you are spraying on their thoughts.

Parents, when they are preparing their girls for marriage from a young age, should also prepare their sons too for adapting to marriages, and having a flexible mindset, supporting a new person in their life and home. Household jobs are not just a girl or a woman's responsibility, but equally the responsibility of a guy or a man.

Parents should teach their male child to respect the woman in their life and not treat them as a house help.

Conclusion

With all our experiences, we don't conclude that all men suck, or their families are useless. It's our misfortune that we came across some exceptional cases. We came across characters who held a qualification and were yet uneducated.

Our education has always taught us - Don't ask for dowry, don't pressurize girls/ women, don't keep them under control. The guys we met, most of them sported an ego or were dominant. Most of them had a lady who ruled their home - their mother - and everything happened as per her wish. The irony is one lady rules the house and another one is unacceptable and seen as a threat, or an intruder.

The arguments start and eventually pressure builds up which affects the newly married bride & groom. The guy is sometimes unable to live up to the expectations of both his new wife and his old parents finally leading to divorce. Marriage is between two people, and it depends how strong they are and how much they trust each other.

Communication has to be clear and concise. There should be no third person between the husband and wife. The couple should be each other's back, or else there would be a fallback.

When the new bride arrives, welcome her, give her space to understand people, culture, and rituals at home. Don't pressurize her with your expectations. The new person will be shocked, withdrawn, and overwhelmed and perhaps not function altogether.

When you resort to asking for dowry, making unsolicited claims, making wrong predictions with horoscopes and birth charts, and hiding information in a marriage, you might marry, however such marriages won't last long. If you feel you are facing all this, stand for yourself and demand what is right for you.

You will come across many people during this journey, you may have many partners in various forms, it is important that you narrow down on what you want from your partner and communicate accordingly.

Pal was clear on what kind of a guy she wanted and kept on rejecting guys who didn't fit in with the mental persona of her partner. Finally, Vinayak came into her life, and he seemed to fit the persona she always had in mind.

Girls have been educated for ages to adjust and live in their in-law's house. This can happen if parents begin inculcating these things in guys at a young age. Guys should be taught to respect every woman, not just their Mom or sister. They should be prepared to help and contribute to every task at home.

Like a girl looks after her in-laws, a guy should be equally or less inclined to support and help his in-laws. He needs to balance both his parents and his bride and keep them both happy. When the partners are compatible, they accomplish their goals together.

Some people get married in their 20s and feel like it is the end of their life because they have no scope or vision beyond that. Others settle down in their 30s and then get married. Some wish to live in, some wish to never get married. There is no right or wrong age for getting married, nor is there a right or wrong age for having children—as long as a woman has her menstruation, she can have children, or she can simply freeze her eggs. When society starts talking about marriage or having kids, young people tend to run away and hide, not because they have done anything wrong, in fact they are tired of dealing with ignorance and constantly having to answer these questions and make people understand.